The
HELICOPTER

AN ILLUSTRATED HISTORY

KEITH CAREY

Patrick Stephens, Wellingborough

© Keith Carey 1986

First published in 1986

British Library Cataloguing in Publication Data

Carey, Keith
The Helicopter.
1. Helicopters—History
I. Title
629.133'352'09   TL716

ISBN 0-85059-795-1

*Patrick Stephens Limited is part of the
Thorsons Publishing Group*

Photoset in 10 on 11pt Plantin by Avocet Marketing
Services Limited, Bicester, Oxon. Printed in Great
Britain by Anchor Brendon Limited,
Tiptree, Colchester, for the
publishers, Patrick Stephens Limited, Denington Estate,
Wellingborough, Northants, NN8 2QD, England.

The
HELICOPTER

Contents

Acknowledgements

I am grateful to the following individuals and organizations for their generous help in providing information and photographs for this book:

The Public Relations and Publicity Department of Westland Helicopters Ltd; Sgt R. L. Tring of the Museum of Army Flying; Mr L. F. Lovell of the Fleet Air Arm Museum; Miss Jane Radford of the Copyright Section Ministry of Defence; Lt Cdr Morgan, RN Public Relations Officer Royal Naval Air Station Yeovilton; Flt Lt C. M. Blenkinsop, WRAF Public Relations Officer RAF Lossiemouth; Royal Air Force Station Odiham; Cdr M. Maddox RN Royal Naval Air Station Lee on Solent; Flt Lt R. J. Lander, 22 Squadron RAF Chivenor; Flt Lt M. P. Ricketts, 22 Squadron RAF Coltishall; Flt Lt R. Bendy 22 Squadron, RAF Manston; the commanding officer of 819 Naval Air Squadron, HMS Gannet; Second Officer Sue Eagles, WRNS Public Relations Officer Royal Naval Air Station Culdrose; Sqd Ldr D. M. Hyman, 22 Squadron RAF Leuchars; Mr J. L. Parsons, 22 Squadron RAF Valley; Helicopter Marketing Ltd; Shell Photographic Library; Hans Burman of Bofors Ordnance; Dollar Helicopters; Court Helicopters (PTY) Ltd; Linda Hill, administration manager, Colt Executive Aviation; Hughes Helicopters Inc; Bell Helicopter Textron; Mr A. J. Leahy, director of administration (pilots), Bristow Helicopters Ltd; Ted Veal of Columbia Helicopters Inc; Mr W. B. D. Wardle, commercial director of FPT Industries Ltd; Ferranti Instrumentation Ltd; John J. Fetsko, president, Spitfire Helicopter Company; Brenda Bourque of customer relations, Petroleum Helicopters Inc; Gill Hopkins of Alan Mann Helicopters Ltd; Mr T. D. Burnal, helicopter sales manager, CSE Aviation Ltd; Kit Chambers of North Scottish Helicopters Ltd; Lesley Smith of Marconi Avionics Ltd; Jill Owen of British Caledonian Helicopters Ltd; Inspector J. W. Saville of the Metropolitan Police Air Support Unit; Ruth Allen of the Metropolitan Police, Public Information Department; extracts from, *Policing From the Air* by kind permission of the Metropolitan Police; McAlpine Helicopters Ltd; Ed Long of Okanagan Helicopters; Rotorway Aircraft Inc; Boeing Vertol Helicopters; Mr Robert C. Ferguson of the Lockheed California Company; Sikorsky Aircraft; British Aerospace Dynamics Group; *The Airtour Gazette*; David George of Sloane Helicopters Ltd; Messerschmitt Bölkow Blohm Gmbh (Munich); Jean Louis Espes, *Attaché De Presse* of Aérospatiale Helicopters; Gary Savage of Alan Mann

Helicopters Ltd; Amanda Bratt of Skyline Helicopters Ltd; Brian Pickering of Military Aircraft Photographs, Department of Photographs of the Imperial War Museum; Associated Kent Newspapers Ltd and the editor of the *East Kent Gazette*.

I would also like to say thanks to the following ...
Basil Pring who taught me to fly
and
Pete 'I eat nails' Shouldis who taught me the helicopter.

Keith Carey
Sittingbourne, Kent, 1986

Chapter 1

Introducing the helicopter

The helicopter, that marvellous invention of a flying machine, is a saver of lives, an oil workers' taxi, a flame-spitting gunship or a collection of spare parts flying in loose formation. The modern helicopter is many things to many people and although its useful development has been rather recent, contributory ideas and thoughts about the possibility of vertical flight date back beyond the fourth century BC in ancient China. In those far-off days Chinese children amused themselves with a little toy whose basic principles, thousands of years later, would enable man to add a new dimension to the science of the air, that of vertical flight. Some two hundred years after those children, Archimedes the Greek of Syracuse, (the word helicopter is derived from the Greek words *helix* meaning 'spiral' and *pteron* meaning 'wing') perfected a form of rotary screw which was used as a water pump. Thousands of years were to pass before it was realized that Archimedes' screw would operate equally well in another form of fluid, that of the air.

In relatively recent history, however, the beginnings of the helicopter are usually associated with the drawings and writings of the fifteenth century Italian artist, philosopher and engineer, Leonardo da Vinci. To label da Vinci as the inventor of the helicopter would be incorrect, for he was in reality only an engineer carrying forward the idea of the ancient Chinese flying top. His well known drawing of a 'helical screw' which he theorized would bore its way through the air via windlass power, is however generally accepted as the first logical design of the basic helicopter concept. It is not known if da Vinvi's 'airscrew' actually flew, but it would seem unlikely as there does not appear to have been any allowance made for the effects of torque and stability.

In the 1780s, an updated version of the Chinese toy top was designed and built by two Frenchmen, named Launoy and Bienvenu. This consisted of two sets of feathered blades contra-rotating at each end of a vertical shaft, powered by a whalebone helically wound bow. Records say it was demonstrated before the assembled scientists of the French Académie des Sciences on 28 April 1784, its unusual flying characteristics arousing a great deal of interest in the august meeting chamber. Thus this small model became the first known heavier-than-air machine to make a successful free vertical flight. Across the English Channel at this time, Sir George Caley, often referred to as the 'father of British aeronautics', was also building models along the principles of the Launoy and Bienvenu machine. Until his death on 15 August 1857, Caley was active in the field of rotary-wing research. He is known to have built several types of helicopter rotor system, some being bench tested by means of a falling weight. Like most of his contemporaries, be they interested in fixed-wing or rotary-wing flight, the single biggest stumbling block was the lack of suitable motive power. Although the steam engine was in existence and indeed powered many non-flying aeronautical models, such engines were too inefficient and heavy to be of practical use in an actual flying machine. Down through the years, however, various other experimental models were built and flown, some capable of a few minutes flight, others staying firmly with mother earth.

It was not until the twentieth century, with the invention of the reliable small petrol combustion engine, that the helicopter in its simplest form as we know it today took its first precarious and wobbly steps into the air. On 19 September 1907, four years after Wilbur and Orville Wright took to the air in their 'Flyer', a Frenchman, named M Volumord, piloted the first helicopter to leave the ground with a man aboard. This machine was the Gyroplane No 1, built by the French brothers Louis and Jacques Breguet, in association with Professor Charles Richet. Constructed of tubular steel, it had four eight-bladed rotors, a total of 32 lift-producing surfaces and was powered by an Antoinette 40 hp piston engine. The machine was very unstable and had to be held at arm height by four helpers on the ground—it cannot therefore be credited with being the first to fly free, a

The Breguet No 2 Gyroplane of 1908. Powered by a 55 hp Renault engine the machine made a number of successful flights during the summer of 1908 but was later severely damaged during a forced landing.

technicality in reality since the ground helpers did not contribute to the lifting power of the rotor. It was however the first helicopter to lift itself and its pilot free of the ground under its own power and must therefore be judged successful. Another Frenchman, Paul Cornu, took over where the Breguet brothers left off. On 13 November 1907 at Coquain-Villiers, near Lisieux in France, the Cornu helicopter with its inventor aboard as its pilot, rose in to the air to a height of a foot or so but only managed to remain airborne for some twenty seconds. Although disappointed at being airborne for so short a time, Cornu and his machine were the first to make a vertical take-off and free flight entirely without assistance or stabilization from tethers or ground helpers.

Powered by a 24 hp Antoinette aircraft engine, the machine was highly unstable—a dominant attribute of rotorcraft design for many years, and this, combined with a shortage of funds, caused Cornu to abandon further development of his historic machine. Virtually no further progress in helicopter design and development was made during the First World War. In 1923, however, a young Spaniard, Juan De La Cierva, achieved a significant step forward in the field of rotary-wing flight when he constructed his first autogyro.

The autogyro is not a 'pure' helicopter, it achieves its thrust through the air in the same manner as a conventional aeroplane, by means of an orthodox engine and propeller. The significant difference is that whilst an aeroplane derives its lift from a mounted fixed-wing, the autogyro obtains its lift from a freely rotating 'wing' or rotor system. In terms of performance, the autogyro can perform some very short, almost vertical take-offs, fly at very slow forward airspeeds and land almost vertically with practically no ground run at all. The essential difference between the helicopter and the autogyro is not always clearly understood. The helicopter's rotor system is driven directly by the engine, the relative airflow being drawn down through the rotor disc to produce lift. The autogyro on the other hand allows its rotor blades to 'freewheel' or 'windmill' in the airflow provided by the forward movement of the machine via the conventional propeller. In the autogyro, the airflow enters the rotor system from below. This principle of 'autorotation' is what gives the helicopter its unique built-in safety factor. The helicopter engine can be disengaged via a clutch from the rotor system, the free wheeling action continues to turn the individual blades of the rotor, thus providing lift under which the helicopter can be flown to a safe landing with complete control. On the autogyro the rotor is not geared to the engine whilst in flight, so unlike the helicopter the autogyro cannot perform hovering manoeuvres, fly sideways or backwards or land vertically.

Cierva's autogyro was none the less extremely valuable to the development and construction of rotor hubs and blades. In some of his early flights, with a rigid rotor hub, Cierva discovered that as the forward speed of the autogyro increased, the amount of lift on one side of the rotor disc increased, while on the other side it decreased, thus resulting in a loss of control. To compensate for this action Cierva mounted the individual rotor blades to the hub by means of a horizontal hinge pin. When tested the extra lift developed by the advancing blade half of the rotor disc could be compensated for by allowing the individual blade or blades to flap upwards via the hinge. This reduced the effective angle of attack of the rotor blade and therefore its lift angle. Meanwhile, the retreating blade half on the rotor disc, its lift decreased by the autogyro's forward motion flapped downward and the lost lift was restored.

This significant development of the rotary-wing system was known as an 'articulated rotor'. To meet the demand for a stronger, safer rotor blade, Cierva again used a hinge. This time it was mounted on a vertical axis, enabling the blade to 'drag' back or move forward relative to the main hub, in other words a 'drag hinge'. To prevent excessive vibration developing in the rotor system as a result of movement around these hinges, Cierva added 'blade dampers' which, like shock absorbers, tend to minimize movement of the individual blades around their hinges. These three elements, developed by Cierva: the flapping hinge, drag hinge and blade damper can still be found in many present-day helicopters.

The true helicopter has been and still is a complicated and expensive machine to design and build. To obtain the required amount of lift for a vertical take-off, it is obvious that the rotor diameter of the helicopter must be far greater than that of the conventional aeroplane propeller. This rotor must also be able to increase its lift on all of its blades at the same time or 'collectively' in order to achieve a vertical ascent. During this change main rotor rpm must be maintained at approximately the same output. To move the helicopter into forwards, sideways or backwards flight from the hover requires a cyclic change in the rotor's plane of rotation.

The cyclic pitch control enables the pilot to change the pitch of each individual rotor blade, thus resulting in the rotor disc tilting in the direction that pressure is applied to the cyclic pitch control stick. If the stick is moved forwards, the rotor

This Cierva C.8V powered by a Viper in-line engine was one of a long series of early autogyros constructed by the Spanish pioneer Juan De La Cierva.

Delivered to the School of Army Co-operation from 1934 onwards the Cierva C30A Autogyro served with 1448 Flight (later re-numbered 529 Squadron) of the Royal Air Force where, known as the 'Rota', the type operated on radar calibration duties.

disc tilts forwards, if it is moved sideways the rotor disc tilts sideways and so on. For example, as the pilot's control stick is moved forward, the angle of attack is decreased as the individual rotor blades pass 90 degrees to the pilot's right and increased as they pass 90 degrees to the pilot's left. Because of the effect of gyroscopic precession, the maximum downward deflection of the blades is forward and the maximum upward deflection is at the rear, thus causing the rotor disc to tilt forward in the desired direction of cyclic displacement. A similar analysis can be applied for any other directional displacement of the cyclic control stick. Now that the rotor system is able to produce controlled lift, another problem confronts us. The engine power results in a turning movement, or torque, which creates a tendency for the fuselage to turn in the opposite direction to that of the rotor. This effect is countered in a single-rotored helicopter by provision of a small tail or anti-torque rotor, the pitch of which can be increased or decreased by means of the anti-torque or 'rudder' pedals in the cockpit to keep the helicopter on a heading parallel to the desired line of flight. In twin or tandem rotor helicopters, the rotor systems rotate in opposite directions thus each cancels out the torque of the other.

These contributions to helicopter design and development resulted in the first machine to have complete controllability, the Focke-Achgelis Fw 61. Professor Heinrick Focke, in association with a fellow German named Achgelis, conducted

Above *Hanna Reitsch at the controls of the Focke-Achgelis Fw 61 helicopter in the 'Deutschlandhalle' Berlin in 1938.*

Below *The Army 'Deutschlandhalle' display team with one of their Sioux helicopters.*

Above *Who needs turboshaft engines when you've got clockwork power!*

Below *During the British Army Tattoo in the 'Deutschlandhalle' in 1973, Hanna Reitsch's performance of 1938 was repeated by a Sioux helicopter of '7' Flight Army Air Corps.*

some useful research into rotary-wing flight during the 1930s. The successful result of this research was the Fw 61, a twin rotor machine with its lifting blades mounted on outriggers either side of the main body. Registered *D-EBVU*, the Fw 61 comprised the fuselage and engine of the Focke-Wulf Fw 44 Stieglitz, a basic training aeroplane. The propeller gave no assistance with forward flight, in fact it was cut down in size merely to serve as a cooling fan for the engine.

With Germany's celebrated female pilot, Hanna Reitsch, at the controls, it made its first free flight on 26 June 1936 and remained airborne for some 45 seconds. On 10 May of the following year, it made its first autorotational landing and in February 1938 for fourteen consecutive nights it was flown again by Hanna Reitsch in the vast Deutschlandhalle sports stadium in Berlin. The degree of control demonstrated by this remarkable helicopter made an intense impression on the vast audience, many of whom were leading Nazis of the day. Although Flugkapitän Reitsch had less than three hours experience on type before the demonstration, the Fw 61 was apparently easy to fly and had few unpleasant handling characteristics. It was later flown from Bremen to Berlin at an airspeed of some 68 mph, another helicopter first of its day.

Across the North Atlantic in America at this time, other helicopter enthusiasts were also hard at work with their own developments. Outstanding amongst these was Igor Sikorsky who was born in Kiev, Russia on 25 May 1889. As a boy he showed great interest in contemporary science, particularly in the field of aviation. While still at school, he constructed and flew several model aircraft made from tissue paper and strips of bamboo. Later during a tour of Germany with his father,

Left *Flugkapitän Hanna Reitsch.*

Right *The great Igor Sikorsky at the controls of the VS-300, one of the first really practical helicopters. In this photograph Sikorsky is seen with the VS-300 in one of its early forms during tethered flight testing*

a psychology professor, during which he first heard of Orville and Wilbur Wright, he came into contact with the works of Count Zeppelin, which more or less decided the direction the young Sikorsky's career would follow. A graduate of the Petrograd Naval College, he studied engineering in Paris before returning to Kiev and entering the mechanical engineering college of the Polytechnical Institute in 1907. In 1909 he returned to Paris, then the centre of European aeronautical knowledge, to learn what he could of the embryo science of aeronautics. While in Paris, Sikorsky met many of the famous men who would later become household names in aviation and announced to them, despite strong advice to the contrary, his plans to design and construct a helicopter. He then returned home to Kiev, taking with him an Anzani 25 hp engine. The first helicopter he built stayed firmly on the ground refusing all attempts to persuade it into the air. A second machine constructed in the following year did little better, it rose a short way from the ground but was not capable of lifting a pilot. Power was lacking at this point in time and with so little known about rotary-wing flight, Sikorsky turned his attention to large fixed-wing aircraft.

After the revolution of 1917, Sikorsky emigrated to France, giving up a considerable personal fortune in the process. There he was employed to build a large fixed-wing bomber for the Allied services. This aircraft was still in its design stage when the Armistice was signed and after unsuccessfully trying to obtain work in the French aviation industry, he left for the United States of America in 1919. Sikorsky appeared to have abandoned the idea of the helicopter, turning instead to the design and production of the first four-engined heavy transports

Igor Sikorsky 1889–1972 is acknowledged as the founding father of today's modern helicopters. Yet Sikorsky did not invent anything, but like Leonardo da Vinci before him he applied an engineer's mind to the best of all the then available knowledge, refined it and came up with the successful VS-300.

and ocean-spanning Clipper flying boats. Around 1931, however, with two careers already behind him, Sikorsky resumed his interest in the idea of rotary-wing flight. In 1938, whilst working as the engineering manager in the Vought-Sikorsky Division of the United Aircraft Corporation, many years of patient research and development came to fruition when the board of UAC gave its permission and backing for Sikorsky to expand his helicopter research. It is sometimes claimed that Sikorsky in fact did not invent anything, and this is probably true in that, like Leonardo da Vinci, he applied an engineer's mind to the best of all the then available knowledge, refined it and came up with the VS-300. The VS-300 helicopter was designed in the spring and constructed in the summer of 1939. On 14 September of the same year, with Sikorsky himself at the controls (he was dressed for the occasion in a topcoat and felt fedora to protect himself from the cold downwash of the rotor) the aircraft lifted off on its first vertical flight.

At this stage the helicopter remained tethered to the ground and in addition had large weights slung underneath to help keep it stable. Igor Sikorsky did most of the development test flying personally in what was then an open welded tubular steel frame with a four-cylinder 75 hp Lycoming air-cooled engine, a power transmission of v-belts and bevel gears, a three-wheel main landing gear and a three-bladed main rotor with a diameter of 28 feet. After some early problems with the cyclic pitch control, which was temporarily discarded, the machine made its first free flight on 13 May 1940, the fuselage configuration having changed with the addition of outriggers at the tail end and increased engine power now supplied by a 90 hp Franklin.

By the middle of 1940 the VS-300 was managing to remain airborne for fifteen minutes at a time, and on 6 May 1941, it broke the world helicopter endurance record, held until then by the German Fw 61 (with a time of 1 hour 20 minutes 49 seconds) by remaining aloft for 1 hour 32 minutes 26.1 seconds. Testing of the VS-300 continued throughout the following year, when after numerous modifications it was demonstrated before an assembled group of US Army and Navy pilots. Outstanding among the early pilots to fly the VS-300 was Captain Franklin Gregory of the US Army Air Corps. In the 1940s Captain Gregory was one of the few licensed military autogyro pilots, and he later became one of the first to fly Sikorsky's helicopter. In his later book, *The Helicopter*, he recalls a kangaroo-like take-off and subsequent flight in which he was convinced that the helicopter was in a class of its own. A major contributory cause of Gregory's trouble was the fact

The controls of the helicopter and their principal functions: 1 Cyclic control stick—controls attitude and direction of flight. 2 Anti-torque pedals—maintain heading. 3 Collective pitch lever—controls altitude. 4 Throttle—controls rpm. 5 Rotor brake—provides smooth gradual engagement of the main rotor system.

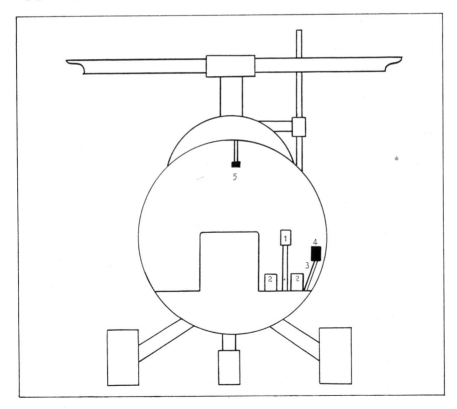

that the VS-300, even after eighteen visibly different configurations, was still underdeveloped and crude. The basic difficulty however, although Gregory was a qualified autogyro pilot, was that a true helicopter is more difficult to fly than almost any other type of aircraft. Now, 45 years later, with computer-assisted controls, stability augmentation systems and autopilots, which enable modern helicopters to be flown with some ease despite most outside weather conditions, the helicopter remains a more complex flying machine than its fixed-wing counterpart, presenting the trainee rotary-wing pilot with a more difficult challenge. Unlike even the smallest fixed-wing aeroplane, which when trimmed out will allow the pilot to concentrate on other things by remaining fairly stable and on its desired heading, the helicopter is inherently unstable. When Captain Gregory made the transition to flying helicopters it required no radical changes in the thinking processes, but it did require the acquisition of new skills and knowledge, which introduce new perspectives to old problems. Automatic fixed-wing reactions will not always produce the same results in a helicopter as they would in an aeroplane. This, therefore, would seem to be a good point to explain the basic controls of the helicopter and give the reader an idea of what each one does. The following controls are discussed in the order in which they are operated to control the helicopter.

The cyclic control

This control stick is the helicopter's equivalent of the fixed-wing aeroplane's control column or 'joystick' and its function is to feather the blades of the main rotor 'cyclically' to control the attitude of the disc in the lateral and longitudinal axes. Because of the effect of gyroscopic precession, the main rotor mast tries to align itself along the axis of the rotor's rotation, therefore providing attitude control over the fuselage of the helicopter as well as the disc of the main rotor. Responses to control inputs of the cyclic are the same as for fixed-wing aircraft, directionally anyway. Cyclic response is very sensitive and quick in all airborne regimes from the hover to fast forward flight. Moving the cyclic control tips the rotor disc, thus directing the lift force in the desired direction and giving the helicopter pilot complete control. The cyclic control achieves roll and pitch control in much the same way as a fixed-wing aircraft's control column. It does not need ailerons and elevators to do this but controls the rotor disc (wing) directly. Proper handling requires small, smooth corrections more in the nature of gentle pressures than actual movements.

Anti-torque pedals

Much the same as rudder bars or pedals in a fixed-wing aircraft, the anti-torque or tail rotor pedals control the pitch of the small tail rotor. The tail rotor blades are set to have positive pitch when in the neutral position to offset torque in stabilized forward flight. If the main rotor blades turn anti-clockwise, an equal and opposite reaction from the power of the engine turning those blades tends to turn the fuselage of the helicopter in a clockwise direction. The heading of the machine is controlled via the pedals as rudder bars or pedals are used in fixed-wing aeroplanes. In a helicopter however, there is no adverse yaw in a turn in forward flight, so that unlike the conventional aeroplane, the helicopter pilot needs no pedal movement to make a co-ordinated turn. Anti-torque pedals are used for 'on the spot' turns and precision work whilst hovering the helicopter. Any change the pilot makes with the collective pitch lever or twist grip throttle will also require a compensating change in anti-torque pedal pressure.

Collective pitch lever
The collective pitch control is operated by the helicopter pilot's left hand and is so called because it alters and controls the pitch of the main rotor blades all at the same time or 'collectively'. It is arranged to work in such a way that when the pilot operates the collective stick, it causes an increase in the angle of incidence of the main rotor blades in relation to the main rotor hub. Increasing collective pitch demands greater engine power because drag from the rotor increases as a function of the angle of attack of the blades. Conversely lowering the collective stick decreases the lift and drag of the rotor and engine power should therefore be reduced to prevent overspeeding the rotor disc. The collective pitch stick is in effect the engine power demand control and as such it is linked to the powerplant through a correlating cam which operates so that when the helicopter pilot lifts the collective stick it opens the throttle and when it is lowered it reduces the throttle. This action helps to maintain the operating rpm of the rotor within acceptable limits. Therefore since the collective pitch control stick influences rpm and the twist grip throttle influences manifold pressure, each is a secondary control of the other's functions. The helicopter pilot must therefore refer to both his manifold pressure and tachometer instrumentation to determine which control to use, and by how much.

Throttle
The throttle has been covered to some extent in the section on the collective pitch lever, where it was established that the throttle and collective whilst in flight must be co-ordinated to maintain the desired rpm and manifold pressure. The twist grip type throttle is mounted on and synchronized with the collective pitch lever. It can be adjusted independently for starting and warm up operations as well as for in-flight adjustments of the engine rpm. With the introduction of gas turbine engines, manual control of engine rpm was changed to automatic control, but the twist grip is often retained as a select control or emergency manually-operated throttle.

Trim control
A switch in the helicopter cockpit, the trim control commands electrically-operated mechanisms on the control linkages that compensate control pressures caused by variables in flight conditions.

Rotor brake
Rather like the handbrake of your motor car, the rotor brake is a small lever in the cockpit which when released provides smooth, gradual engagement of the rotor

system. It is also used to control the main rotor in high gust conditions, such as on the flight deck of an oil platform or warship.

Friction locks
These usually come in the form of a small ring or screw located on the main helicopter controls and enable the pilot to adjust the hand pressure of the various controls to his individual requirements. They can also be used to lock the controls in any desired position.

★   ★   ★

By 1944, Gregory had made the first helicopter airmail flight, the first touchdown on the deck of a moving ship and the first non-stop flight by helicopter from Washington DC to Dayton, Ohio. In 1941, the US Army Air Corps awarded a contract to Sikorsky Aircraft to build an experimental helicopter to be known as the model XR-4. The Sikorsky XR-4 or VS-316A was a further development version of the VS-300 and gained the distinction of being the first helicopter in the world to enter continuous production. Like the VS-300, the fuselage was constructed of welded steel tube, but it was now fully covered by fabric apart from a small area by the tail rotor. The cockpit was fully enclosed in plexi-glass, providing accommodation for two persons and fitted with dual flying controls. Almost twice the size of the VS-300 it was powered by a 165 hp Warner R5003 engine and took to the air for the first time on 14 January 1942. On 18 May 1942, after being handed over to the United States Army Air Force, it flew in several easy stages to Wright Field, Ohio, a distance of some 761 miles (1,225 km) from Bridgeport, Connecticut, and taking some sixteen hours in flying time. It is said that during this five-day delivery flight the helicopter emerged from being an experimental development to a fully fledged aircraft. By 1943, several Sikorsky R4s had seen service in many different terrains from the Burmese jungle to the snowy wastes of Alaska and notched up a list of other notable achievements including the first ever landing by a helicopter on a ship at sea.

One hundred production aircraft were ordered by the USAAF of a type essentially similar to the R4 but fitted with a more powerful engine and increased range. The type also saw service with the US Navy, where it was known as the HNS-1 and with the US Coast Guard. Approximately 45 were supplied under lend-lease arrangements to the United Kingdom, some going to the Royal Air Force where they became known as the Hoverfly 1 and replaced the Rota autogyros of 529 Squadron. Most however were to serve with the Royal Navy's Fleet Air Arm, where the type was used for Fleet requirements and pilot training. The Sikorsky R4 did not have a long military career on either side of the Atlantic, being replaced in the early post-war years by the S-51 and its Westland-built equivalent, the Dragonfly.

At the same time as Sikorsky was developing his machine another American, Arthur Young, designed an experimental helicopter for the Bell Aircraft Corporation in Buffalo, New York. Although the United States was soon to be drawn into the Second World War and the Bell Corporation would be producing fighter aircraft in previously undreamed of numbers, the president of the company, Larry Bell, made time to talk with Arthur Young and sound out his ideas on rotary aviation. Bell quickly saw that the future development of the helicopter could be big business even though its immediate future would have to be delayed because of the impending war. Larry Bell hired Arthur Young and with a small team of dedicated staff they worked in a small garage in a Buffalo suburb for eighteen months to produce the first Bell helicopter, the Model 30.

The work was privately funded by Bell and no government or military contracts or sponsorship were sought. The design conceived by Arthur Young had two very important innovations that were utilized in the helicopter that he was building then and which are still in use on the Bell helicopters of today. The most striking feature of the Bell Model 30 was its two-bladed main rotor. It was a semi-rigid type connected to the cyclic and collective controls but the main hub was not articulated. There were no flapping or drag hinges, instead was the second important innovation. This was a stabilizing bar mounted at 90 degress to the main rotor blades, some five feet in length and with streamlined weights mounted at each end. This stabilizer is a patented device still to be found exclusively on Bell helicopters today. It rotates with the shaft at right angles to the blades and tends to maintain its own plane of rotation independent of both the shaft and of the main rotor. Interconnected to the control system it has a stabilizing influence on the rotor disc.

These Sikorsky R-4 helicopters are under test at the factory in America before delivery to the Royal Navy.

In September 1943, Larry Bell announced that his corporation would enter the field of commercial helicopter production although at this time the Model 30 was not even licensed.

The first of an initial batch of ten Model 47B, two-place helicopters, with a 178 hp Franklin engine was flown on 8 December 1945. The Federal Aviation Administration type approved certificate was issued to this aircraft on 8 March 1946, the first ever awarded to a commercial helicopter anywhere in the world. This machine had cost the Bell Corporation some $12 million to develop, and, whilst Bell himself was not an engineer, he was able to inspire others to invent and build their ideas into flyable machines. Over 5,000 units of the Bell 47 in more than sixty different versions have been constructed by Bell Helicopter and foreign licensees: Westland in Great Britain, Agusta in Italy and Kawasaki in Japan. Most Bell 47 Models have been developed for the military services and used for training, observation and utility roles. Familiar to many people from the American television series *MASH* the casevac version of the Bell 47D or H-13E as it was known, was used in substantial numbers in the Korean War, the first armed conflict in which the helicopter played a major role. Although a relatively small and underpowered aircraft, the H-13E could carry two stretchers or casualty litters mounted externally and saved many lives by quickly evacuating wounded troops from the front line to mobile surgical units. Civilian versions of the Bell 47 are still in widespread use around the world today, employed in all aspects of aerial

The Bell model 61 or HSL-1 was Bell's only tandem rotor helicopter and although not a successful aircraft the type did see service with the US Navy in the 1950s. A number of these helicopters were to have been delivered to the British Fleet Air Arm under the Mutual Defence Assistance Program, but when the Korean War ended the order was cancelled.

work from pilot training and crop-spraying to powerline patrol and survey work.

After outstanding success with the Model 47 and its variants, the Bell Company moved on to a more ambitious project, a purpose designed tandem rotor anti-submarine hunter-killer aircraft for the US Navy. The result, although not an outstanding helicopter in its own right, was designated the Bell Model 61 or HSL-1. In June 1950, this helicopter was announced as the winner of the US Navy's design competition and a preliminary order for a batch of three evaluation aircraft was placed. It was the first and only Bell helicopter to be constructed with a tandem rotor layout. Intended to operate from small platforms aboard ship, it was designed to carry submarine detection equipment, autopilot, a comprehensive radio fit and de-icing equipment. Weapon loads could include bombs, depth charges or air-to-surface missiles and with an operating crew of two pilots and two aircrewmen, but the challenging ASW/hunter/killer role proved to be too difficult a mission to be accomplished and the fifty production aircraft delivered to the US Navy, out of an ordered total of 78, spent much of their time as troop transports or training aircraft. Under the Mutual Defense Assistance Program some eighteen aircraft were scheduled for delivery to the Fleet Air Arm, but the Korean conflict had drawn to a close by the time the HSL-1's development programme had been completed and the order was cancelled.

Back around 1943 in Philadelphia, the first of Frank N. Piasecki's helicopters was unveiled to the world. This was a single rotor type, fitted with an anti-torque

At the small end of the rotary wing table are the small autogyros or gyrocopters such as this Benson machine. A small engine of around 72 hp drives a pusher propeller and the slipstream coming up through the rotor disc (unlike a true helicopter which draws the air down through its rotor) pushes or 'autorotates' the blades.

tail rotor and designated the PV-2. The first demonstration of its capabilities to the military went off well, but Piasecki wanted to demonstrate further a more practical use for his machine. With some journalists and photographers in attendance, he pulled the PV-2 from a friend's garage, unfolded the rotor blades into position and took off from the driveway. A few seconds later he floated down beside the gas pumps at a nearby filling station, filled his tank with three gallons and took off again this time heading for the local golf course. Alighting near the first tee, Piasecki took his golf clubs from the baggage compartment and teed off!

In the early years of the post-war era in America, people dreamed of a typical family standing in their backyard waving to father as he lifted off in his private helicopter heading to his place of work downtown. After successful demonstrations, the US Navy awarded a contract to Piasecki on 1 February 1944, to develop and build an initial batch of three tandem-rotor rescue and utility transport helicopters. This was the beginning of the Piasecki Helicopter Corporation. Designated the HRP-1 Rescuer and forever known as the 'Flying Banana' because of its shape, it had a modest service career and was in its time the world's largest helicopter. Powered by a Wright R975 piston engine it made a successful first flight in March 1945 at Morton, Pennsylvania. The test programme was completed by the spring of 1947, when work had already begun on an initial production batch of ten aircraft for the US Navy. These production models were powered by a Pratt & Whitney R1340 ANI engine and twelve were later delivered to the US Marine Corps for assault duties, while three others went to the US Coast Guard as HRP-1Gs for rescue work. Later, in the 1950s, Frank

This Vertol HUP-2 Retriever served aboard large warships and aircraft carriers of the US Navy during the 1950s on search and rescue, plane guard and general utility duties.

Piasecki sold his shares in the corporation and the name of the company changed to the Vertol Corporation, which later became a division of the Boeing Company, being known as the Boeing-Vertol Company. Frank Piasecki moved on to form the Piasecki Aircraft Corporation and turned his aeronautical engineering skill to the design of missile, aircraft and electronic components. Also designed was a high-speed compound research helicopter known by the name of Pathfinder. Developed as a private venture, the Pathfinder was first flown on 21 February 1962. At this stage it was not a true compound machine having no wings fitted, an unfaired cockpit and its retractable undercarriage locked down. A fully enclosed cabin and small folding stub wings were added later that same year. Subsequently, Piasecki was awarded a joint US Navy/Army contract to develop a compound helicopter capable of research into flight speeds of up to 230 mph (370 km/h).

Another of the younger emerging helicopter designers was nineteen-year-old Stanley Hiller. At the tender age of just fifteen, young Stanley was the successful business head of Hiller Industries, a small company grossing over $100,000 a year from the sales of small toy racing cars powered by model aircraft engines. He built and crashed his first helicopter, the co-axial rotored XH-44 single seater in 1944. Within three months it had been repaired and gave a public flying demonstration on San Francisco's Marina Green. Hiller then managed to obtain a small loan from the Bank of America and set up shop by forming United Helicopters Incorporated, with manufacturing premises in an old wine warehouse. At a later date, the company built its own plant at Palo Alto in California by raising more backing and from the sale of some public stock. With the co-axial design

The Vertol model 43 or H-21 was produced in a number of models and variants and the type served with various military and civilian operators in the late 1950s and 1960s.

abandoned in favour of the single-rotor type helicopter, the Hiller Model 360 was certified in October 1948 and was the first machine available for under $20,000.

In the Model 360 Stanley Hiller introduced a system just as revolutionary as the stabilizing bar Arthur Young had perfected for his Bell helicopters. Hiller patented his 'Rotormatic' system, which had two control paddles mounted on short arms at right angles to the main rotor blades. In effect, the pilot flies the paddles and the control paddles fly the helicopter. On 12 April 1949, Stanley Hiller, after a 5,200-mile flight around North America, landed the Model 360 on the doorstep of a banking firm in Wall Street, New York, which had turned down his request for a loan to build the machine! It was around this time that the Hiller company merged with Fairchild to become the Fairchild-Hiller Corporation.

In Great Britain, Raoul Hafner at the Bristol Aeroplane Company began design studies into the type 171, later known as the Sycamore. Intended to conform to Ministry of Supply Specification E20/45, the prototype machine, powered by a 450 hp Pratt & Whitney R985 Wasp junior radial piston engine took to the air for the first time on 27 July 1947. The certificate of airworthiness for the 171, the first to be granted for a British-designed helicopter was awarded on 25 April 1949. The Sycamore served in many harsh climatic conditions with various military units. The United Kingdom's Army Air Corps took delivery of the HC 10 and 11 liaison and ambulance version, Coastal Command of the Royal Air Force evaluated the

A Sycamore helicopter lands at Lynmouth during the 1952 flood disaster there.

type for communications and search and rescue work and in later service operated them in Cyprus, Aden, Kenya and Malaya. Other operators of the Sycamore included British European Airways, who took delivery of two, the Royal Australian Navy, Royal Australian Air Force, West German Army, West German Navy and the Royal Belgian Air Force.

Encouraged by the success of the 171, Hafner's team designed and built two prototypes of a new tandem-rotor transport helicopter to meet Ministry of Supply Specification E4/47. This was to be Bristol's first twin-rotor machine and utilizing the cockpit, rotors and dynamic parts of the Sycamore; the first type 173 Mk 1, as it was known, flew on 3 January 1952. Powered by two Alvis Leonides 550 hp nine-cylinder piston engines with seating for two crew and ten passengers it embarked on HMS Eagle for sea trials. Although successful helicopters for their day, they were dogged by bad performance, a result of the unavailability of the intended turboshaft powerplants. Derived from the Type 173, the Type 191 was to have been the dedicated anti-submarine version for the Royal Navy. Intended to be powered by two Napier Gazelle turbines, it was, however, after much argument, cancelled in the 1957 Defence White Paper and replaced with the Westland Wessex, a licence-built version of the Sikorsky S-58.

The Royal Air Force continued with the Type 191's developed as a tactical

The Westland Sycamore 4/5-seat light helicopter was designed and built by the Bristol Aeroplane Company in the late 1940s.

transport helicopter and with a stretched fuselage and different landing gear this became known as the Belvedere. As a transport for eighteen fully-equipped troops it was totally unsuitable owing to a very cramped cabin and internal access which was almost non existent. Development was still not complete when the pre-production machines were delivered to the Service Trials Unit at Royal Air Force Odiham in Hampshire in October 1960. With a ridiculously short airframe life of only 1,600 hours the first Belvederes were delivered to No 66 Squadron, Royal Air Force, in September 1961, followed by No 26 and 72 Squadrons in 1962. With a two-man operating crew the Belvedere was theoretically designed to lift between 18-25 fully-equipped combat troops or twelve stretchers depending on range to be flown. Internal cargo load was up to 6,000 lb (2,722 kg) and an external slung load of up to 5,250 lb (2,381 kg) could also be lifted. The type served in Aden, Africa, Borneo, Malaya and the United Kingdom before it was withdrawn from RAF service in March 1969.

The turning point in making a helicopter a viable proposition from both the military and commercial standpoint came in the 1950s, when Sud Aviation, now known as Aérospatiale, fitted an Artouste turboshaft engine to its Alouette light helicopter. This new powerplant no longer made the banging and ripping sound of the old piston engines when starting—instead it emitted a high-pitched whistle or shrieking sound like that of a jet aircraft, but it did offer reduced vibration and better performance. When this machine was first flown on 12 March 1955, the French gained a commanding lead in European helicopter technology and went on to sell over 1,300 variants of the Alouette to military and civilian customers all over the world. Not only are turboshaft engines more powerful than piston powerplants, they are smaller, more efficient, easier to maintain and use a safer fuel. An average piston powerplant requires expensive high octane gasoline, the turbine on the other hand will happily operate with a wide range of fuels which are not only cheaper, but can be found in general use with civilian and military aviation operators at airfields all over the world. These fuels include various gasolines and kerosenes, though if necessary household paraffin, ships' oil and even commercial heavy lorry diesel fuel can be used.

Before the innovation of turbine powerplants, a number of helicopter operators, notably Sabena and British European Airways in Europe, and Los Angeles Airways in North America, introduced passenger and air mail carrying services utilizing piston-powered machines such as the Sikorsky S-55 and S-58. Although the commercial operators and airlines were out to make a profit, the helicopter services they set up were of an educational nature rather than a serious business proposition and were financed or subsidized by some other aspect of the airline's operation or by direct government subsidy. Later with the

Right *The Westminster was a large helicopter produced for research and first flew in 1958. As a transport the machine could have lifted 45 fully-armed troops and flown them at a speed of 150 mph (240 km/h) for 100 miles (160 km). Several flying crane applications were projected for the Westminster similar to those flown today by the Sikorsky S-64 Skycrane. When the Westland company took over the Rotodyne and Fairey Aviation, the project was abandoned.*

appearance of large transport types such as the tandem-rotor Boeing Vertol 107 and Sikorsky S-61L which, among others, both operated with New York Airways, helicopter operating costs at last began to look feasible.

Almost every advance that has been made in the field of helicopter design and development has been accomplished in meeting some military requirement. From the Korean War came the Bell 47, seemingly constructed from a Meccano set, a saver of lives, darting around the combat zone plucking wounded soldiers to safety. In the 1960s with the Americans becoming deeply involved in the Vietnam conflict, some very advanced hardware was leaving the manufacturers' assembly lines and finding its way into US Army Air Cavalry units. The Hughes OH-6A Cayuse known as the Model 500 to civil operators, was the winner of the US

The Westland Belvedere HC Mk 1 was the first twin-rotor, twin-engined medium lift helicopter to serve with the Royal Air Force. Entering service in September 1961, the Belvedere served in many parts of the world notably in Brunei, Tanganyika and the Radfan operations. The aircraft in this photograph is preparing to lift an underslung dismantled Wessex helicopter from a jungle clearing.

The tandem-rotor Boeing Vertol 107.

Army's Light Observation Helicopter (LOH) competition. Twelve American helicopter manufacturers entered various designs and from these one each was selected from Bell, Hiller and Hughes. The Bell entry, designated HO-4, was eliminated almost straight away, leaving the Hiller and the Hughes. In November 1964, the Hughes OH-6 began flight trials at the US Army Aviation Center, Fort Rucker in Alabama. Pronounced the winner in May 1965, some 1,434 units were ordered and delivery to the US Army began in September 1966. In Vietnam, the Hughes OH-6 was nicknamed 'Loach' from the letters LOH and it operated as the scout aircraft in a hunter/killer team with the Bell Huey Cobra known as the 'Snake', the 'Loach' acquiring the target, the 'Snake' coming in for the kill.

Also prominent in the war in South-East Asia were rotary-wing giants such as the Boeing Vertol Chinook and the Sikorsky S-64 Skycrane. Again the result of a US Army competition, the Model 114 or Chinook as it later became known was selected as the standard battlefield mobility helicopter. By June 1965 armed CH-47 Chinooks were being evaluated under combat conditions in Vietnam with the US Army's 1st Air Cavalry Division. They were mounted with 40 mm grenade launchers, 20 mm cannon and five 0.50-calibre window-mounted machine guns. The fuselage of this helicopter was a box like interior 7ft 6 in (2.28 m) wide, 6 ft 6 in (2 m) high and over 30 ft (9.2 m) long. By the early 1970s more than 550 of these helicopters had seen combat duty in Vietnam, mainly as a battlefield transport flying in troops and artillery weapons but also serving as a combat rescue machine which on one occasion became a champion in rescue circles by lifting 200 refugees from danger in a single lift.

Sikorsky's first crane helicopter, the S-60, was a piston-engined research vehicle built from funds shared between the parent company and the US Navy. From this evolved the S-64 Skycrane which took to the air on 9 May 1962. After evaluation at Fort Benning, Georgia, the US Army placed its first order for the type in June 1963. Operated with the 478th Aviation Company in support of the 1st Air Cavalry Division, the CH-54 or Tarhe as it is known in military service is credited with retrieving over 380 downed American aircraft from behind enemy lines in Vietnam, saving a claimed total of $210 million. There is no actual fuselage on this helicopter, instead a structural beam supports the engines, landing gear and tail rotor. Palletized containers or boxes can be clipped underneath and in this manner a complete field hospital, 48 casualty stretchers or some 67 fully-armed troops can be transported, although on one occasion a Tarhe in Vietnam successfully lifted some 87 combat soldiers in a single lift. The type is scheduled for withdrawal from US Army Reserve in the late 1980s.

Other helicopters familiar in the South-East Asia theatre were the Sikorsky Jolly Green Giant and Kaman Huskie: the former achieving fame for behind-the-lines rescues of downed pilots and for deep penetration raids by special forces (such as the abortive raid on the Son Tay prison camp), the latter serving as a crash rescue helicopter, ready to operate as a crash rescue truck, able to fly to the scene of an accident or crash and suppress the flames with its rotor downdraught while

Right *In service with Okanagan as a flying crane helicopter this Sikorsky S-61L is employed on logging operations and the aircraft in this photograph can be seen with an underslung log on its way to the mill.*

Below *This Sikorsky S-61L is flying miners to the Edson coalfield in Alberta. This particular helicopter is operating on the Luscar Coal Company passenger contract which ceased following the closure of their Edson mine in May 1983. Since the contract started in May 1977 Okanagan carried some 750,000 passengers on some 35,000 flights. The two Sikorskys involved, C-FDKB pictured here, and sister ship C-GJDR, have since returned to Vancouver.*

toting rescue crews and chemical bottles. But if any one aircraft could be said to have drawn the attention of the public to the helicopter it is the Bell UH-1 or as it is more universally known the 'Huey'.

The 'Huey' was to the war in Vietnam what the jeep was to World War 2. This particular helicopter has been built in larger numbers than any other aircraft except for the Soviet Anatov AN-2 biplane transport. In service as a multi-role utility and transport helicopter, there was practically no job to which the Huey could not be and was not assigned. As a casevac or 'dustoff' aircraft it saved countless lives and as a gunship it paved the way for the specialized Bell Model 209 or Huey Cobra attack helicopter. With the Vietnam war over, large numbers of casevac Hueys were assigned to MAST (Military Assistance to Safety and Traffic), its main mission being quick reaction to highway accidents, something the helicopter can fulfil with ease whenever traffic clogs the ground. Bell Hueys are also operating in civilian form in the oilfields of the Gulf of Mexico, North Sea, Alaskan North Slope and elsewhere as an airborne bus to transport workers to remote and often inaccessible sites.

In all aspects of helicopter development from relatively early machines up to today's modern aircraft, the single largest limiting factor to further development has been the speed of the main rotor system in forward flight. With conventional technology, current helicopters have reached a practical maximum forward speed of little more than 200 mph (322 km/h). This is dictated by a number of variable factors such as advancing blade compressibility, the stall of the retreating blade, offset torque, drag and so on. Although compound helicopters and their variations

The Aérospatiale SA 316 Alouette 3 is a highly successful light military helicopter and is seen here in French Army markings.

9540

The OH-58 or 'Kiowa' was the runner up to the Hughes OH-6 'Cayuse' in the US Army's Light Observation Helicopter contest in 1962. In 1968 however the Army purchased large numbers of the OH-58 and the type saw substantial active service in Vietnam.

go some way to relieving this problem with wings to offload the main rotor during flight and auxiliary propulsion units to provide extra thrust, they are at best a stop-gap measure or substitution. Progress to surmount this problem is currently proceeding along the lines of rigid rotor research and with tilt-rotor aircraft. By adopting a rigid rotor the helicopter will have a number of advantages over a similar aircraft fitted with a fully-articulated system. The primary feature of the hingeless or rigid rotor system is the removal of the lagging and flapping hinges.

Current rotor research is being conducted by Sikorsky's high-speed S-69 or ABC (Advancing Blade Concept) aircraft and it has been under contract to the US Army Air Mobility Research and Development Laboratory. A two-seat research aircraft, the S-69 is equipped with two contra-rotating rigid rotors which eliminate the risk of retreating blade stall at high forward speed by ensuring that the majority of the load placed on the rotor disc is carried on the advancing blade half of each rotor. This means that stub wings to offload the rotor system in forward flight and the provision of an anti-torque tail rotor and its associated transmission system are not required. When it was considered that the necessary testing as a pure helicopter had been completed, a pair of Pratt & Whitney turbojets were mounted on the helicopter in fuselage pods to supplement the helicopter's main power unit. Various test combinations are underway with this helicopter and it is hoped to take the speed level to around the 345 mph (555 km/h) mark.

Sikorsky has another helicopter employed on rotor research, the S-72. Officially known as the RSRA (Rotor Systems Research Aircraft) two initial prototypes of this helicopter have been built for a trials contract with NASA and the US Army, and they are used for evaluation and development of a range of integrated engine and rotor systems. With fixed wings and turbofan engines, the S-72 is used in compound research as well as for testing various reverse velocity, composite bearing-less, variable geometry and jet flap rotor systems. Together with the Bell XV-15 tilt-rotor research aircraft which takes-off vertically like a helicopter and then at a safe height rotates its twin rotors through up to 90 degrees to fly forward like a conventional fixed-wing aircraft, these may prove to be the helicopters of the future. For the moment these designs appear to show some promise and if, and when, these or similar types enter production, helicopter technology will step over a barrier that has been blocking its path for many years.

Right *A US Army CH-47D Chinook with an underslung howitzer and ammunition pack.*

Below *The Hughes OH-6A Cayuse was an outstanding US Army light observation and scout aircraft known as the 'Loach' during the Vietnam War. Most were flown, as here, with the doors removed, this facilitated exit from the helicopter in case of a crash and also aided pilot visibility.*

Above *This Hughes OH-6 is from the US Army's former helicopter display team the 'Silver Eagles'.*

Top right *The Sikorsky S-64 Skycrane helicopter.*

Bottom right *This piston-engined Sikorsky S-58 is in service as a flying crane.*

Below *Diagram of the CH-47D Chinook layout.*

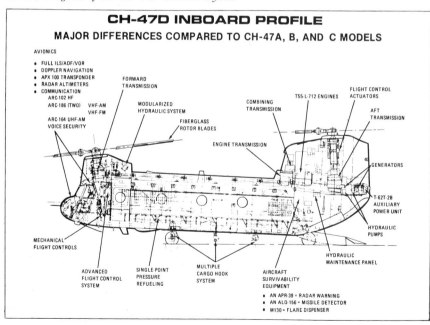

CH-47D INBOARD PROFILE
MAJOR DIFFERENCES COMPARED TO CH-47A, B, AND C MODELS

Left *The Sikorsky S-64 or CH-54A 'Tarhe' as it is known to the US Army, is an efficient flying crane helicopter. Special containers can be fitted to the fuselage, as in this photograph, to carry freight, troops or a wide variety of cargoes.*

Centre left *A Sikorsky CH-53D shipborne heavy assault transport of the US Marine Corps.*

Bottom left *The Kaman HH-43B Huskie was a single-engined inter-meshing rotor configuration helicopter which served with the Air Rescue Service of the US Air Force and was specially designed to operate as an airborne fire and crash rescue machine.*

Below *The Sikorsky S-72 or Rotor Systems Research Aircraft (RSRA) is a high-speed multi-purpose research helicopter under contract with the US Army and NASA.*

Bottom *The Army/Navy/NASA/USAF/Sikorsky S-69 or XH-59A is an Advancing Blade Concept (ABC) research helicopter built for testing rotor systems in high speed forward flight manoeuvres.*

Above *The Bell model 301, or XV-15 as it is more widely known, is a tilt rotor research aircraft. In operation the aircraft takes off vertically the same as a helicopter and then at a safe height, the rotors are swivelled through some 90 degrees to a horizontal position ready for transitioning into forward flight. In this photograph the aircraft is seen during sea trials operating from the USS* Tripoli.

Below *A pioneer in the field of rigid rotor aircraft, the Lockheed-California Company's CL-475 helicopter has been donated to the Smithsonian Institution's Air and Space Museum. The CL-475 first flew in 1959 and was used to demonstrate the rigid rotor principle to officials of the Federal Aviation Administration and all branches of the military services. It paved the way for later generations of rigid rotor craft with greatly increased performance as compared with conventional helicopters.*

Chapter 2
Helicopters in uniform

A famous General once said that the military commander's most pressing requirement was 'to see the other side of the hill'. Over the years in order to meet that requirement servicemen have climbed trees, scaled buildings, ascended in balloons and flown light observation aircraft. With the advent of the helicopter however, tactical battlefield observation advanced tremendously, providing the field commander with a highly versatile and relatively fast vantage point from which to direct his units on the ground.

The helicopter first began to wear military uniform in the later part of the Second World War. The Sikorsky R4 or Hoverfly 1 of the American Forces, although it did not see operational front line service, was used in the rear areas of theatres such as the Philippines, Okinawa, New Guinea, Burma and Europe. The first helicopters to see operational service were those of the German armed forces, in particular those designed by Anton Flettner. Flettner's early design work was often overshadowed by the efforts of his contemporaries, Igor Sikorsky and Heinrich Focke. In spite of the well documented achievements of these two designers and their machines, Flettner's first helicopter, the FL 265, flew several months before Sikorsky's VS-300 and was far superior to Focke's twin-rotor helicopter, the Fw 61. The FL 265 first flew in May 1939, the prototype being fitted with a contra-rotating intermeshing rotor system. In spite of a preliminary order for six of these machines, Flettner knew he was capable of producing a better helicopter and by the end of the summer of 1940 he had refined the FL 265 into the FL 282 Kolibri or Hummingbird.

The FL 282's maiden flight took place in 1941 and the German Navy ordered thirty prototypes and fifteen pre-production aircraft. The first three prototype aircraft were completed as single seaters, the remainder becoming two seaters with accommodation for a pilot in front and an observer at the rear. Like the FL 265, the FL 282 underwent demanding pre-service trials prior to unit service. At least twenty Kolibris saw operational service, usually operating from hastily constructed platforms above the gun turrets of convoy escort ships. They flew on anti-submarine, reconnaissance, scouting and re-supply duties in the often extreme weather conditions of the Baltic, North Aegean and Mediterranean Seas. By the end of the war, however, only three of the 24 prototype aircraft completed survived, the remainder being destroyed to prevent their capture by the advancing Allied Forces. Of these one found its way to the Soviet Union, the other two going to the United States. Among other early rotary-wing designs under German development were the Focke Achgelis FA 223 Drache and the Doblhoff WNF 342. The Drache or Dragon, was an advanced helicopter for its time and was in a way a larger and improved version of the Fw 61. Powered by a 1,000 hp Bramo Fafnir 323Q-3 piston engine, it was intended to be the standard utility transport helicopter for the Luftwaffe. An order for one hundred production machines was placed but before deliveries could begin, Allied bombing destroyed all but a handful. One of the survivors was flown across the English Channel in September 1945 to the Airborne Forces Experimental Establishment at Beaulieu in Southern England. Its life in the United Kingdom was not long however as it was destroyed on its third test flight when control was lost after a vertical take-off.

The Doblhoff WNF 342 was the work of a three-man design team, Friedrich Von Doblhoff, Theodor Laufer and A. Stepan. This particular helicopter was unique in that it was the world's first to take off and land using tip-jet propulsion to power its main rotor. Intended to meet a requirement for a small observation helicopter, the basic airframe was altered in shape several times. Doblhoff had found that the tip-jets consumed a prohibitive amount of fuel, particularly whilst hovering so he installed a BMW Bramo radial piston engine and propeller for forward flight and let the rotors 'freewheel' thus saving fuel for the take-off and landing. There were several other designs prevalent in Germany at the end of the war but with the Allied Forces advancing on Berlin, many were destroyed to prevent their capture. With the Second World War drawing to a close and the remains of German industry decimated by heavy bombing, many of Germany's leading rotary-wing designers went to the United States where their expertise was instrumental in helping the Americans build up a successful post-war helicopter industry.

During the war, when the helicopter was still in its infancy, only two types of tactical assault had been available to the battle planners: frontal and flank. But in 1946, officers of the United States Marine Corps (USMC) began to initiate a long range programme of evaluating battlefield helicopter techniques. The helicopter was but a crude vehicle when forward thinking USMC officers envisioned it as a means of tactical dispersion, not deterred by the fact that at the time the machines available could carry little more than a pilot and a single passenger.

Towards Korea

In the early post-war years, helicopters were increasingly finding their way into military units, with the US Air Observation Post squadrons being among the first to replace their light aircraft with the new rotary-winged machines. The Sikorsky R6, for example, which made its first flight on 15 October 1943, was a refined and developed version of the Sikorsky R4 using the same rotor and transmission system as that aircraft. Powered by a 245 hp Franklin piston engine, the R6 began to resemble the sleek modern lines of today's machines with its streamlined metal skinned fuselage and moulded plexiglass cockpit. The majority of these

Above *Hoverfly 1 aircraft from No 43 Operational Training Unit formate for the camera.*

Below *The Flettner FL 282 'Kolibri' with contra-rotating, twin intermeshing rotors was the only true helicopter to see active operational service during the Second World War. By the end of the war however, only three of the 24 aircraft constructed survived, the remainder being destroyed to prevent capture by the Allied Forces.*

helicopters were constructed by the Nash-Kelvinator Corporation and a production contract for over 190 of these machines was started in 1945. Most were delivered to US Naval units, where they were employed mainly on air and sea rescue duties.

A number of R6 helicopters were also delivered to Great Britain, like the R4 before it, under lend-lease arrangements. Principal users were No 657 Squadron RAF and the Airborne Forces Experimental Establishment (AFEE) at Beaulieu. The first two R6s arrived in this country in April 1947 and were assigned to 1901 Flight, 657 Squadron, where they were quickly joined by a further four machines. The Hoverfly 2 as the helicopter was known in British service did not have a long military career as it was little better than the R4 Hoverfly 1, despite its more modern appearance. The engine was still underpowered and the helicopter itself was prone to becoming unstable, largely through rotor imbalance. Although the helicopter was operated in support of Army artillery exercises it was decided not to introduce the type into widespread squadron service. This turned out to be a wise decision as shortly afterwards lend-lease arrangements with the United States came to an end and spare parts for the R6 became virtually unobtainable.

Around this time in South-East Asia, tension was mounting and culminated in the North Koreans invading the South across the 38th Parallel at dawn on 25 June 1950, thus beginning the Korean War. It was quickly established that aircraft would be needed particularly in the liaison, artillery spotting and casevac roles. For the first few months of hostilities however there were no helicopters available,

This Focke Achgelis FA 223 'Drache' was an advanced helicopter for its time, but before delivery of the type could begin Allied bombing destroyed all but a handful. The aircraft in this photograph is the second prototype, D-OCEW, seen here undergoing acceptance trials in 1942.

Above *Hoverfly 1, KK995/E, at RAF Andover, the home of No 43 Operational Conversion Unit.*
Below *A Sikorsky R-6A Hoverfly 2 of 657 Air Observation Post Squadron flying at Larkhill in 1947.*

and these tasks were being performed by obsolete and often unserviceable light aircraft. The first US Army helicopters in Korea did not arrive until December 1950. These were Bell H-13s with the primary role of observation and liaison although a small number of aircraft did operate with the 2nd Army helicopter detachment at Seoul for casevac duties. This unit in its first month of operation evacuated over 500 casualties from the battle zone earning each of the pilots the Distinguished Flying Cross. In addition to the H-13, Hiller 360s and Sikorsky H-5 and H-19s were also in widespread use in Korea.

The Sikorsky H-5 was twice as powerful as the Bell H-13, but still carried only the same two casualty stretcher load, although these were in specially constructed pods or panniers, protected from the elements and unlike the open litters of the Bell. Most of the H-5s in Korea were assigned to combat rescue duties and pulled off many dramatic rescues of airmen downed behind enemy lines. These rescue flights saved the lives of 9,680 men and over 966 of these were rescued from behind enemy lines.

A typical mission occurred on 10 March 1951, when the three Flights of F-80 Shooting Star fighters were assigned a ground attack sortie near the Taedong River area, behind the North Korean lines. At first, the mission went well as the jets thundered low over the 38th Parallel en route to the target. When they reached the Taedong River, the individual flights came in one by one to attack the target, a small but important bridge. The American jets instantly drew heavy ground fire, but repeatedly pressed home their attacks. Disaster struck as the third Flight completed its attack run, the leader's wingman was hit by anti-aircraft fire and although he struggled to keep control of the badly-damaged jet, he lost altitude fast and was forced to eject. While the other two Flights returned to base, the remaining three aircraft of the third Flight orbited overhead on a rescue Combat Air Patrol (CAP) in case any Communist forces should appear on the scene.

An hour after the distress message was sent, a Sikorsky H-5 helicopter arrived at the scene. By this time, a number of North Korean troops were approaching the area and closing rapidly on the downed American pilot. A swift cockpit conference took place between the chopper pilot and the orbiting jets. It was decided that the helicopter would fly directly to a spot on the ground where the pilot could be seen hiding, while the fighters kept the enemy troops' heads down with their machine guns. As the Shooting Stars flew over for their strafing run, the H-5 moved in for the pick up. The helicopter soon drew considerable small arms fire and there was a strong risk of a vital component being damaged and the enemy being able to take the helicopter crew prisoner as well. The F-80s, though, were performing their role well and the Communist troops were kept at bay whilst the downed pilot was snatched aboard the helicopter. The H-5, although badly holed and losing fuel, was able to make it safely back to American lines and so saved a valuable pilot to fly and fight another day.

By the early part of 1952, however, the H-5s were becoming obsolete and most were replaced by Sikorsky H-19 helicopters. The H-19 powered by a 600 hp Pratt & Whitney R-1340-57 Wasp radial piston engine had an increased operating range and a larger cabin accommodating some 8-10 persons. These helicopters were soon able to demonstrate their worth as H-5 replacements when, in July 1952, part of the United Nations front line was covered by freak floodwater. Several United Nations units were forced to leave their positions and make for higher ground where the US Air Force H-19s lifted them out of the danger zone. In addition to carrying out these rescue duties, their ability to operate from almost any patch of level ground saw them increasingly used for observation, liaison and troop transport duties. This capability was soon noticed by troop commanders on the spot, for the helicopter needed no roads and could supply forward units with men, weapons and food in places no land transport could reach. During the Korean conflict, this technique of airlifting troops into the battle zone was perfected by the US Army and Marines.

Some Sikorsky H-19s even had standard issue bazookas strapped on the aircraft's side and the crewman fired them by pulling a long cord that extended from the trigger mechanism into the cabin. The results, of course, were crude and accuracy was an unheard of thing, but the enemy troops who were used to taking pot shots at the slow unarmed helicopters received quite a surprise. Although the US Army did not begin to equip its helicopters as weapons of war for several more years, the realization that the vulnerable chopper could fight back was not lost and in less than a decade when American troops would again go into action in South-East Asia, in the Vietnam war, the armed helicopter or 'gunship' would be as instrumental in the land battle as the infantryman or the tank.

The Malayan Emergency

While bitter fighting continued in Korea, the British were using their helicopters in a variety of roles in the dense tropical jungle of Malaya. After the war with Japan had ended, British troops returned to Malaya, and the resident guerrilla forces which had had very little effect against regular Japanese troops, agreed to disband. The British administrators then began to introduce political legislation, particularly on voting rights which immediately proved unpopular, the differing racial groups of Malays, Indians and Chinese each resenting the others having a say in the government's affairs. After two years of constant strikes, protest and negotiation these new laws were abandoned. The strikes continued however and new legislation was passed which made the strike illegal. Violent rioting continued and the guerrilla or 'Malayan Peoples' Anti British Army' rose against the government and a state of emergency was declared.

With the difficulties of jungle warfare, the value of the helicopter was quickly appreciated in Malaya with aircraft being requested for the specific task of casualty evacuation. The Royal Air Force back in the United Kingdom at this time was not equipped with any suitable helicopter type and so the request was passed on to the Royal Navy which released three of its Westland-built S-51 Dragonflies to the Air Force. In May 1950 these aircraft were shipped to Malaya and formed into a unit known as the Far East Air Force Casualty Evacuation Flight, the Royal Air Force's first such unit. In almost three years of existence this Flight, which operated from the Royal Naval Air Station, Sembawang, airlifted some 265 casualty cases.

At first these rescues were very much hit and miss affairs as no one, least of all the helicopter pilots, was sure how the machines would cope in conditions where the temperature was often 100°F with 100 per cent humidity; frequent tropical storms ensured the additional hazard of torrential rain and severe turbulence. Not least of all was the problem of the jungle itself, with its canopy over 200 ft above the ground. The first recorded rescue by a helicopter from this unit was on 15 June 1950 when, after a train ambush near Labis, a soldier of the King's Own Yorkshire Light Infantry was evacuated from a waterlogged airstrip at Segamat and flown to hospital in Singapore. Compared with later operations this first casevac was highly conventional.

A common type of casevac in Malaya would take place as follows. When a request for assistance reached headquarters, an Army Auster Air Observation Post (AOP) aircraft was despatched to locate the relevant patrol, often operating deep into the jungle, and contact the commander over the radio. Having ascertained the extent of the casualty's injuries, the Auster would then locate a suitable clearing and direct the patrol to it. Alternatively if a clearing suitable for a helicopter to land could not be found, explosives or chain saws were often dropped with instructions on how to prepare the site. At this point, the patrol commander would have to make a decision whether it was quicker to clear a landing zone or march out of the jungle. In most cases however the extent of the soldier's injuries and the difficulty of the terrain precluded the latter choice. The Dragonfly's limitations were soon apparent however and it was realized that larger types capable of troop transport as well as casevac duties were needed.

With the Korean war in full swing at the same time as the Malayan Emergency the demand for helicopters was tight. The Americans at this time, although supplying British Forces with aircraft under the Mutual Defense Aid Pact, would not condone their use in 'war' conditions. Therefore a Royal Navy unit, 848 Squadron equipped with ten Whirlwind HAS 21s from the carrier HMS *Perseus*, was diverted for use in Malaya. These aircraft were painted a distinctive midnight blue and were flown ashore to be stationed at Kuala Lumpur and within a few days of their arrival were flying their first missions. Much of 848 Squadron's work in Malaya involved troop re-positioning, reconnaissance, target marking, leaflet dropping and artillery positioning.

The naval pilots rapidly became familiar with the Malayan landscape and built up a special relationship with the Army Auster AOP pilots of 656 Squadron who had been in Malaya from the start of the conflict. The Army Austers often flew with the casevac helicopters, acting as navigational leaders and sometimes providing top cover while the helicopter set down for its pick up. The Army pilots had an uncanny knowledge of the supposedly featureless jungle, where to the untrained pilot one tree looked much the same as another. They were particularly skilful in picking out suitable clearings for the helicopter to land in and often dropped instructions to ground patrols on how to prepare them. The helicopters of 848 Squadron were also used by the Special Air Service for parachuting duties, where the chopper conferred a special advantage to the troopers by enabling them to exit in a compact area, essential in areas known to be active with terrorists. The

Special Air Service troopers were usually dropped from around 600 ft and upon landing in the jungle canopy, a dangerous task in itself, dropped ropes and abseiled down to the jungle floor.

On a number of occasions the Whirlwinds themselves were forced to land in the jungle through engine failure or a similar malfunction. The first time this took place, in a rice paddy, the aircraft began to sink in the mud and was dismantled on the spot and flown out in five missions by another 848 Squadron machine. The fuselage, rotor head, tailcone, gearbox and lastly all the bits and pieces in a canvas bag were all lifted out to fly another day. In its first year of Malayan operations 848 Squadron lifted out some 10,000 soldiers and over 225 casualties. In January 1954, 848 Naval Air Squadron was awarded the 'Boyd' trophy for its outstanding work.

As the Malayan Emergency continued into 1960, the number of helicopters operational in the Far East for troop lifting and casevac duties increased. The first all-British machine to serve in the theatre was the Bristol 171 Sycamore designed by Raoul Hafner. This machine joined 194 Squadron Royal Air Force in Malaya in 1954 and despite initial problems with its wooden rotor blades in the humid tropical conditions it went on to give sterling service throughout the remainder of the conflict.

While the British were building experience with the Whirlwind in Malaya, its Sikorsky-constructed brother, the S-55, was being delivered to the French Armed Forces under the Mutual Defense Aid Pact of 1953. The French expeditionary force at this time was engaged in bitter fighting with the Viet Minh in Indo-China (now Vietnam). Although there was a desperate need for helicopters, particularly in the casevac role, very few S-55s reached the French troops. This lack of troop-carrying helicopters may be directly responsible for the unhappy history of that war-torn corner of South-East Asia. Towards the end of the Indo-China conflict the French garrison was surrounded at a small airstrip at Dien Bien Phu, the only aircraft capable of casualty evacuation had been destroyed by Viet Minh artillery fire and French helicopters were not available in sufficient numbers to play a decisive part. If greater numbers of S-55 helicopters had been operational, the outcome of that unhappy battle might have been different, the French could have been airlifted out to fight another day and stability in the area might have been achieved.

Algeria and Suez
Barely had the rumblings of one war ceased than in November 1954 the French found themselves at war again, this time in the stifling heat of the Algerian mountains. There would be no shortage of helicopters as there had been at Dien Bien Phu: from the first days of the war choppers were used in the assault role because the mountainous terrain was considered too risky for paratroopers. Despite treacherous up currents of air and terrorist snipers the Sikorsky S-55s proved themselves to be able machines although hot and high density altitude conditions meant that each helicopter could lift only five fully-armed troops in place of its normal complement of ten. In addition to the S-55, the French also

operated the Bell 47, the Vertol H-21 Shawnee transport and the Sikorsky S-58 in Algeria. France purchased ninety S-58s directly from Sikorsky and Sud Aviation (now Aérospatiale) built over 166 machines under licence for the French Army Light Aviation (ALAT) and the Aéronavale (Navy).

The French found the Sikorsky S-58 a valuable mover of troops, casualties, ammunition and almost anything else. They also found that guns could be mounted on helicopters, bolted on to the sides to fire directly ahead or fixed to fire obliquely down. Machine guns were also mounted in doorways and manned by a gunner to provide manually aimed firepower. One of the most effective new weapons however was the wire-guided missile. This was directed to its target by electronic signals from an operator in the helicopter's cockpit via a thin copper wire which reeled out behind the missile in flight. Initially intended for anti-tank operations these Nord SS 11 missiles proved very effective against the Algerian terrorists in their mountain bunkers.

While the French continued operations against the Algerians, a battle in which once again they would be the losers, a joint Anglo-French task force landed at key positions in the disputed Suez Canal Zone. On 5 November 1956 British and French paratroops captured the outskirts of Port Faud and Port Said. As soon as the paratroops had secured the airfields around these positions, Whirlwind helicopters from two Royal Navy aircraft carriers HMS *Theseus* and *Ocean* began ferrying in supplies and evacuating wounded troops. The following day, 500 men of 45 Commando Royal Marines were ferried ashore in a mix of Whirlwinds and Sycamores, the first helicopter-borne assault in history.

Although the Suez operation was a political disaster, as a military operation it

The Saunders-Roe Skeeter was a simple helicopter that served in the light observation and training roles with the British Army, RAF, West German Luftwaffe and Marineflieger. The aircraft in this photograph are British Army Air Corps machines.

must be judged a success. The Royal Navy was impressed with the helicopters' role during the operation and went on to form specialized commando assault squadrons, equipped them with helicopters and embarked them on special ships called commando carriers, which were, in reality, helicopter carriers.

The British Army joins in

The British Army decided that it needed aviation support on a larger scale than had previously been supplied by the Royal Air Force or Royal Navy and decided that there would be a significant advantage in operating large helicopters of its own for troop transport and re-supply duties. In 1957, the War Office was directed to become responsible for the operation of its own light aviation and general liaison flying and to this end it was decided to form an Army Air Corps (AAC) which would operate and control its own light aircraft and helicopters provided their all-up weight did not exceed 4,000 lb. This would mean that the Royal Air Force would operate the larger helicopters such as the Whirlwind and Sycamore whilst the AAC would run its own Auster light aircraft and the then new Skeeter light helicopter. Thus, on 1 September 1957, the Army Air Corps officially came into being, taking as its headquarters the former RAF station at Middle Wallop in Hampshire, the largest grass aerodrome in Great Britain. RAF fitters still maintained the Army's aircraft and continued to do so until the Royal Electrical and Mechanical Engineers (REME) had trained enough of their own personnel to take over.

In 1957, Army aviation was essentially a fixed-wing force equipped mainly with the Auster. The Skeeter was introduced to operate in partnership with the Auster in front line units until the early 1960s. Although a delightful helicopter to fly it was underpowered and plagued with mechanical troubles. Constructed by Saunders-Roe, this pretty two seater had originally been a Cierva design and during its initial development stages, the Skeeter was beset by a number of problems. The Skeeter 2 powered by a Gipsy Major 10 145 hp piston engine disintegrated through ground resonance during testing. The Ministry of Supply pressed ahead however and ordered two prototypes of the Skeeter 3 powered by another new British-designed engine, the 180 hp Blackburn Bombardier. These machines were rejected by the Ministry but the talents of the Saunders-Roe designers (the Cierva company having been taken over by the former in January 1951) came up with another version of the aircraft, the Skeeter 5. This was the first version of the helicopter to be almost free of the ground resonance problem which had beset the earlier designs.

By 1956, the Skeeter 6A powered by a Gipsy Major 201 200 hp engine at last began to show signs of proving acceptable, and indeed after pre-service trials deliveries of the type, designated AOP Mk 12, began to the Army Air Corps. Some were fitted with dual controls and were used by the RAF to train helicopter instructors for the Army. Production of the Skeeter ceased in 1960, by which time Saunders-Roe had been absorbed into the Westland Aircraft Group. After mixing the helicopter with the Auster, it was deemed desirable to equip all Army aviation units with one type of aircraft. The helicopter which the Army needed was to be strongly built, able to survive in the field, be reliable and easy to service. The new helicopter was also to be a five seater, offer worldwide operating performance and be compact and no larger than the Skeeter.

Saunders-Roe had already been working on what they termed a 'Super Skeeter' and this seemed to meet most of the requirements for the new aircraft. Two private venture prototype machines were completed and known as the Saro P 531, the first taking to the air on 20 July, the second following it on 30 September 1958. Powered by a Blackburn Turmo 603 turboshaft, the P 531 used a number of components from the Skeeter particularly the wheeled undercarriage, tailboom and rotor assembly, although the P 531 rotor had four blades in place of the Skeeter's three. When the Westland Group acquired the Saunders-Roe company, it took development a stage further by building two more prototypes with, among other changes, a more powerful engine, a skid undercarriage and a rear stabilizing fin. A firm order for the type was placed in September 1960 by the British Army, who would know the type as the Scout AH Mk 1.

Unexpected production delays, largely due to engine problems, held up the Scout's introduction to service and as a stop-gap measure sixteen Alouette 2s were purchased by the Army in 1961 from Sud Aviation of France. The Alouette proved so successful as a 'get up and go' helicopter with little or no mechanical problems that it soon became a firm favourite with pilots and groundcrew alike. Reliable and simple to maintain it was an ideal battlefield helicopter and although the Army would have liked to acquire more of them, the political masters at the

A Skeeter Mk 50 of the West German Luftwaffe.

Ministry of Defence forbade further purchases. Nevertheless the type remains in service in small numbers in 1985.

The Scout when it eventually entered service proved to be an admirable replacement for the Skeeter. It has served both at home and abroad on liaison, utility, casualty evacuation and training duties. It was soon obvious however that the Scout was not going to be suitable for all the roles for which it was originally intended. It was heavier than the Skeeter, difficult to move on the ground and much more expensive than originally planned and the intention of making it the Army aviation units' sole equipment would be financially prohibitive. Liaison and observation flying was clearly to remain an AAC task and to employ the Scout in this role was not thought practicable. For a number of years, trials were conducted with a number of light helicopters and autogyros but because of their inability to operate in all weathers and their limited operating range none was found suitable.

In 1964, flying trials were arranged at Middle Wallop to find a light general purpose utility machine, with a seating capacity for two to three persons and offering worldwide operating performance. Four helicopter types were evaluated: the Brantly B2, the Hughes 300, the Hiller 12E and the Bell 47G-3B1. The Ministry of Aviation drew up evaluation tests based on the qualities that were thought to make up the tactical performance of an Army aircraft. These included handling near the ground, engine power available, hovering ability, tactical concealment and so on. The idea behind these tests was that the best tactical

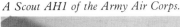

A Scout AH1 of the Army Air Corps.

aircraft would receive the highest score. The winner was the Bell 47G-3B1, narrowly beating the Hiller 12E, its big advantage over that helicopter being its power available in ground hovering manoeuvres. The Sioux, as it was to be known in British Army service, was acceptable to the politicians who would pay for it because although the initial batch of fifty helicopters were to be constructed in Italy by Agusta, the bulk of the aircraft would be built in the United Kingdom by Westland Helicopters Ltd at Yeovil.

Sioux helicopters have served all over the world and almost anywhere that British Army units have been stationed. For example, helicopters have played an important role in Northern Ireland since the start of the present troubles. In 1969, before the present conflict began, the AAC had six Sioux helicopters stationed with the resident battalion, the 17/21 Lancers. Before long these were augmented with a flight of Scout helicopters. By June of 1972, with no let up in the violence, more and more helicopters were allocated to the province and commanders at the time stated that no matter how many aircraft they were given, work could always be found for more. The tasks AAC aircraft are allocated in Northern Ireland include aerial photography, casevac work, reconnaissance patrol and snap vehicle check points. This last involves a helicopter with a number of fully-armed troops stopping suspect cars, the helicopter landing beside the road while the troops check the driver's identification and movements. Helicopters in Ulster are also operated at night, when equipped with a 'Nightsun' lamp, a powerful search light with a focusable white light or infra red beam, they can be used to track suspects on the ground or to light up an area for another aircraft to land in.

The United Kingdom's Army Air Corps has an instinctive feel for the

An early Scout prototype on intensive flying trials.

The cockpit of the Westland Scout AH1.

situations troops find themselves in on the ground and this is important since almost all the UK's battlefield helicopters are operated by the Army. Army aircrew are a cross mixture of full time career aviators and those from other regiments who after completing a year-long training course, serve a three-year tour on flying duties. This continual influx of soldiers from various regiments, particularly from infantry, artillery and cavalry regiments, ensures a high level of fieldcraft among crews and it is this knowledge which is mainly responsible for protecting helicopter crews from enemy fire.

It seems strange but it is true, that no sooner has one helicopter entered service than plans are afoot to replace it. As the Scout and the Sioux settled into their various roles, the Directorate of Land/Air Warfare was drawing up plans for the next generation of Army aircraft to succeed them. It was now very clear that the Army required a utility helicopter to replace the Scout, something which could lift 8-10 fully-equipped troops or alternatively a one ton payload. This was something the Army had been after for a considerable time. The other projected replacement was for a light helicopter no larger than the Sioux, but with a five-seat capacity and greater speed and overall operating performance to be brought in for use in the observation role. Fortunately at this time, Westland Helicopters and Aérospatiale were already working on the Anglo-French helicopter programme to build three types of helicopter—the WG 13 Lynx, the SA 341 Gazelle and the SA 330 Puma. As a result the Lynx became the new utility and anti-tank aircraft, taking over that role from the Scout, and the Gazelle came in to replace the Sioux as the standard rotary-wing trainer, observation and general purpose light helicopter.

The gunship or armed helicopter was developed by the French Army in Algeria but refined by the US Army in Vietnam. In the United Kingdom, helicopter weapon trials were conducted during the 1960s, with a variety of armaments including machine guns both fixed and door mounted, free flight rockets and cannon, although of those tested none were found to be really suitable for the slow-flying Scout helicopter. The massive threat posed by the number of tanks and armoured vehicles of the Warsaw Pact Forces however left the AAC in no doubt that a suitable guided missile was needed for anti-tank operations. To this end, the Army purchased a quantity of Nord SS 11 wire-guided missiles from France and fitted them along with the Ferranti AF 120 optical sight into the Westland Scout. After realistic testing against armour under combat conditions a number of Scout utility helicopters were converted to the anti-tank role and fitted with four of the SS 11 missiles. The present generation of anti-tank helicopter is the Westland Army Lynx, replacing the Nord missile is the Hughes TOW (Tube Launched Optically Tracked Wire Guided) missile. It is envisaged that the partnership of Gazelle and Lynx helicopters will serve British Army Aviation into the mid-1990s.

The forerunner of the Scout was the Saunders-Roe P 531. The prototype first flew in July 1958 and was powered by a 325 shp Turbomeca turboshaft engine.

Above *The Westland Scout was sold to a number of overseas operators—the aircraft in this photograph being operated by the Jordanian Air Force.*

Below *Admired by the British Army as a 'get up and go' aircraft, this Alouette 2 served with No 6 Flight at Netheravon the Army's second UK airfield, although in this photograph the machine is seen at Middle Wallop.*

Below *An Army Air Corps Alouette 2 with an underslung load.*

Right *The Sioux was the British Army's standard light observation and training helicopter for many years before replacement with the Gazelle AH1. The aircraft in this photograph is an Agusta-built machine which served with the Advanced Rotary Wing Flight at Middle Wallop.*

Bottom right *The Westland Sioux was sometimes known to its Army aviators as the 'Clockwork Mouse'.*

ARMY'S "BLUE EAGLES" ON DISPLAY

Above *In March 1968, following requests to Army Aviation units from show organizers a decision was made to form a helicopter display team specially for the purpose of giving displays. The name 'Blue Eagles' was evolved by Colonel R.M. Begbie, commandant of the School of Army Aviation and was adopted in 1968. Its success led to Ministry of Defence agreement that the team should be properly established. Aircraft were specially allotted but were standard Sioux AH Mk 1 apart from electric smoke generators and a light blue livery. Normally there were six pilots each year including the leader and the flying display took a standard form of manoeuvres carried out according to a programme which was supported by a ground commentator describing the helicopters' movements. In spite of the high recruiting value of the team both to the Army Air Corps and the Army generally, the 'Blue Eagles' were disbanded for financial reasons at the end of the 1976 season.*

Below *An Army Gazelle fitted with the AF 532 observation sight hovers just above the tree line.*

A student helicopter pilot and his instructor fly Gazelle AH1, XW 849, past the control tower at Army Air Corps Centre Middle Wallop, the home of Army flying.

Above *These Gazelle AH1s are seen during a typical cross-country training sortie. In actual tactical operations Army helicopters rarely operate above 20 ft of altitude over the battlefield and regularly fly underneath power cables.*

Below *Standard light observation and training helicopter of the British Army is the Gazelle AH1.*

Above *The Westland/Aérospatiale multi-role Lynx helicopter is in service with the British Army. In its anti-tank role a variety of weapons can be fitted or it can be used to transport anti-tank teams to the battlefield. The Lynx is powered by two Rolls-Royce Gem turboshaft engines and is able to carry ten troops or 1,500 kg of freight in its main cabin.*

Below *The crewman of this Army Lynx is directing the pilot into lifting an underslung load of a Somerton-Rayner Sabateur.*

Below *Close up of the AF 532 observation aid showing operator's sight and hand controller.*
Right *A 7.62-mm gattling type 'minigun' installed in the doorway of a Lynx utility helicopter.
The ammunition is belt-fed from a roof-mounted magazine.*
Bottom right *The air-gunner of this Westland Scout has just fired a Nord SS11 wire-guided
missile and is directing it to its target via the Ferranti AF 120 stabilized sight mounted in the
roof.*

Vietnam

When US Forces went into action in South Vietnam the helicopter was an established battlefield delivery vehicle. Large numbers of Bell utility Hueys were in service with the South Vietnamese forces as tactical assault machines, flying troops directly into the area of battle. The biggest drawback to these operations was that in the hostile air over the battle zone the vulnerable and unarmed Hueys were vulnerable to ground fire. It was not until the early 1960s that it was realized that armed helicopters escorting troop-carrying and casevac aircraft could cut down casualties by keeping the enemy's head down with suppressive fire while the heli-borne soldiers were disembarked.

The theory was fine, but the US Army at this stage did not possess a dedicated armed attack helicopter and so improvisation was the name of the game. The Bell UH-1B was among the first to undergo conversion, being fitted initially with machine guns and grenade launchers. This first gunship went on to achieve widespread combat use and was also the first to carry the name 'Cobra'. Powered by a 1,100 shp T53-L-11 turbine and cruising at around 85-95 mph, experience soon showed these helicopters were extremely valuable in escorting troop-carrying machines such as the Sikorsky CH-34 Choctaw. The success of these operations ensured that it was soon Standard Operating Proceedure (SOP) for a standard section of three Hueys to be accompanied by a gunship. Although the armed Huey was providing some protection on escort missions it was obvious that it was but an interim solution.

This Bell 'Huey Cobra' close support and attack helicopter is the twin-engined AH-1J version of the US Marine Corps and is known by that service as the 'Sea Cobra'.

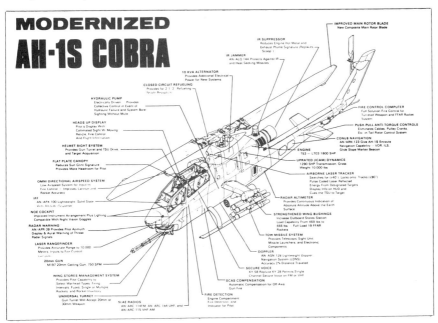

MODERNIZED AH-1S COBRA

IMPROVED MAIN ROTOR BLADE
New Composite Main Rotor Blade

IR SUPPRESSOR
Reduces Engine Hot Metal and
Exhaust Plume Signature (Replaces
Scoop)

IR JAMMER
AN ALQ 144 Protects Against IR
and Heat Seeking Missiles

10 KVA ALTERNATOR
Provides Additional Electrical
Power for New Systems

CLOSED CIRCUIT REFUELING
Provides for 2 1 2 Refueling

HYDRAULIC PUMP
Electrically Driven - Provides
Collective Control in Event of
Hydraulic Failure and System Bore
Sighting Without Mute

HEADS UP DISPLAY
Pilot s Display With
Collimated Sight W- Moving
Reticle Fire Control
And Flight Information

HELMET SIGHT SYSTEM
Provides Gun Turret and TSU Drive
and Target Acquisition

FLAT PLATE CANOPY
Reduces Sun Glint Signature
Provides More Headroom for Pilot

OMNI DIRECTIONAL AIRSPEED SYSTEM
Low Airspeed System for Input to
Fire Control - Improves Cannon and
Rocket Accuracy

IFF
AN-APX 100 Lightweight Solid State

NOE COCKPIT
Improved Instrument Arrangement Plus Lighting
Compatible With Night Vision Goggles

RADAR WARNING
AN-APR 39 Provides Pilot Azimuth
Display & Aural Warning of Threat
Radar Signals

LASER RANGEFINDER
Provides Accurate Range to 10 000
Meters Inputs to Fire Control

20mm GUN
M197 20mm Gatling Gun 750 SPM

WING STORES MANAGEMENT SYSTEM
Provides Pilot Capability to
Select Warhead Types Firing
Intervals Fuzes Single or Multiple
Rockets and Rocket Inventory

UNIVERSAL TURRET
Gun Turret Will Accept 20mm or
30mm Weapon

SLAE RADIOS
AN-ARC 114/FM AN-ARC 164 UHF, and
AN-ARC 115 VHF AM

FIRE CONTROL COMPUTER
Full Solution Fire Control for
Turreted Weapon and FFAR Rocket
System

PUSH-PULL ANTI-TORQUE CONTROLS
Eliminates Cables, Pulley Cranks,
Etc. in Tail Rotor Control System

CONUS NAVIGATION
AN/ARN-123 Give AH-1S Enroute
Navigation Capability - VOR ILS
Glide Slope Marker Beacon

ENGINE
T63 — L703 1800 SHP

UPRATED (ICAM) DYNAMICS
1290 SHP Transmission Gross
Weight 10 000 lbs

AIRBORNE LASER TRACKER
Searches for (±40°) Locks onto Tracks (±90°)
Pulse Coded Laser-Reflected
Energy From Designated Targets
Display Info on HUD and
Cues the TSU to Target

RADAR ALTIMETER
Provides Continuous Indication of
Absolute Altitude Above the Earth
Surface

STRENGTHENED WING BUSHINGS
Increase Outboard Stores Station
Load Capability From 469 lbs to
666 lbs - Full Load 19 FFAR
Rockets

TOW MISSILE SYSTEM
Provides Telescopic Sight Unit
Missile Launchers and Electronic
Components

DOPPLER
AN ASN 128 Lightweight Doppler
Navigation System (LDNS)
Accuracy 2% Distance Traveled

SECURE VOICE
KY 58 Replace KY-28 Permits Single
Channel Secure Voice on FM or VHF

SCAS COMPENSATION
Automatic Compensation for Off-Axis
Gun Fire

FIRE DETECTION
Engine Compartment
Fire Detection and
Indicator for Pilot

Above *Diagram of the Bell AH-1S 'Modernized' attack helicopter.*

Below *The Bell model 249 is a modernized version of the AH-1S 'Huey Cobra' attack helicopter and fitted with the advanced rotor system of the Bell model 412 transport aircraft. It has reached airspeeds of 170 knots.*

The US campaign in Vietnam soon revealed the need for a faster, better armed helicopter than the Huey, one capable of attack as well as defence and so the US Army initiated a crash programme to find such a vehicle. The Bell company back in the United States was already developing an armed support helicopter in the shape of the Bell 207 Sioux/Scout. This was a tandem seat derivative of the Bell Model 47. First flown in September 1963, it was fitted with a TAT 101 gun turret with twin 0.30 calibre machine guns and powered by a Lycoming TVO-435 260 hp engine. This aircraft proved to be underpowered and a production version was never built, instead development continued along the lines of the Bell Iroquois design and this helicopter was proposed and accepted by the US Army in 1965.

The prototype Iroquois aircraft first flew on 7 September 1965 and employed the rotor system and transmission of the UH-1C Huey. The main difference from the earlier aircraft was the extremely thin fuselage which was again fitted with tandem seating and this made the Huey Cobra a much more difficult target in the air. This prototype was sent for pre-service trials to Edwards Air Force Base which resulted in two pre-production AH-1G Cobras being ordered in April 1966. Only days later a confirmed order was placed for 110 aircraft, a total that had climbed to over 838 by 1968. The improvement the Cobra made over the Huey in Vietnam was enormous. On a typical sortie the Cobra could reach its target in half the time of that taken by the Huey, loiter in the combat zone for twice as long and deliver over twice the firepower. Armament could be varied to suit the mission but a sample of typical weapons included an undernose turret fitted with a six barrelled 7.62-mm minigun, two 40-mm grenade launchers and nineteen 2.75 in HEAT (High Explosive Anti Tank) rockets. The greatest advantage that the Cobra had over the armed Huey was that in addition to flying escort missions, it could also be used in the purely offensive attack role.

The Hughes OH-6A and the Bell Huey Cobra were operated together in Vietnam as a hunter/killer team, sometimes known as the 'Pink Team', the OH-6A carrying out a low level search of suspected enemy paths and trails, flying low and fast whilst the Cobra gunship guarded its partner, providing suppressive firepower and relaying radio messages for the 'Loach' (OH-6A) when it was 'screened' by hills or trees. Although the helicopter had demonstrated that it could survive in a hostile sky, casualties among helicopter crews were high, particularly amongst Loach pilots where attrition rates were over 20 per cent in some cases. When flying in this hunter/killer role it was often the hunter that attracted the heavy ground fire and many pilots were shot down several times although on most occasions both they and their aircraft were recovered.

A typical 'Loach and Snake' mission occurred in July 1972 along the Saigon River. A Hughes OH-6A was working its way along the river bank looking for signs of enemy activity when suddenly what seemed like the whole jungle opened up with heavy calibre machine gun fire. An estimated group of thirty Vietcong soldiers had been about to cross the river when the Loach helicopter came into view. His aircraft riddled with bullet holes, the pilot pulled the helicopter into a steep climbing turn out over the trees and away from the danger zone as quickly as possible. The Vietcong troops, meanwhile, did not hang around in the area: past experience taught that American helicopters hunted in pairs and that a Cobra gunship could not be far away. The Loach had been severely damaged and was leaking aviation fuel fast, but before breaking off the engagement and heading for home, the pilot called up his Cobra partner over the radio and vectored him in on the target area. As the Vietcong soldiers dispersed they still offered sporadic small arms fire, but now the Cobra was in the area and flashed overhead putting down a salvo of 70-mm rockets and machine gun fire from its nose turret. Although a number of bodies were later sighted it is not known how many were hit as the jungle was too dense for further action, but once again the Cobra had proved itself worthy of its Vietcong nickname 'The Muttering Death'.

Gunship development

While the Bell company were working on the development prototype to replace the improvized Huey gunships in Vietnam, the US Army had decided to fund a competition for a purpose designed Advanced Aerial Fire Support System (AAFSS). Over a dozen American helicopter manufacturers competed for the contract which was eventually short-listed to two companies, finally going to the Lockheed Corporation in March 1966. Initially ten development aircraft were to be constructed and the first of these, now known as the AH-56 Cheyenne, flew for the first time on 21 September 1967.

The Cheyenne was a tremendous advance over the Bell Huey and Huey Cobra, being intended for day and night offensive missions, reconaissance and anti-armour strike in addition to escort duties. Compared with rival attack helicopter designs the Cheyenne was a big aircraft with a fuselage length of 54 ft 8 in (16.6 m), a height of 13 ft 8½ in (4.18 m), a stub wingspan of 26 ft 8½ in (8.14 m) and a main rotor diameter of 51 ft 3 in (15.62 m). Power for the Cheyenne was a 3,925 shp General Electric T64-GE-16 turboshaft engine turning a rigid rotor system with a solid titanium hub and all metal honeycomb bonded blades. Additional forward propulsion was provided by a pusher Hamilton Standard three-bladed propeller mounted at the rear of the tailboom next to the anti-torque tail rotor and stub wings to offload the main rotor system during flight. During fast forward flight, almost 90 per cent of the Cheyenne's engine power was diverted to the tail propeller. The cockpit was a tandem seat affair, the co-pilot/gunner in the front and the pilot/aircraft captain in the rear. This sophisticated machine was equipped with many special devices including Doppler radar, autopilot, stabilized crew seating, inertial navigation systems, terrain following radar, day and night sensors and a variety of weapons including a 7.62-mm nose turret, 40-mm grenade launcher, Hughes TOW missiles and 70-mm free flight rockets, all weapons incidently being sighted via the on-board computer.

In January 1968, the US Army signed a contract to take delivery of 375 Cheyennes to be ready for service introduction in the early 1970s. In the spring of 1969, however, this contract was cancelled in spite of some impressive test results, due to a multitude of technical and financial problems. The costs, it would seem, were just too much even for the US Army's mighty budget. Although the future development of the Cheyenne is unlikely, the Lockheed Corporation is

Above *Photographed during Nap of the Earth (NOE) operations at the US Army's Yuma proving ground, this AH-56 'Cheyenne' was taking part in demonstrations of its effectiveness in a simulated battlefield environment and its ability to survive hostile anti-aircraft fire.*

Below *Forerunner of the Lockheed 'Cheyenne' was the two-seat CL-595 which was designated the XH-51. Three of these helicopters were built for evaluation by the US Army/Navy and NASA.*

Above *A development AH-56A 'Cheyenne' lets fly with a salvo of 70-mm free-flight rockets over the Hunter-Liggett military testing reservation near King City, California.*

Below *The Lockheed AH-56A 'Cheyenne' was an Advanced Attack Helicopter (AAH) designed during the 1960s. It was intended to become the standard US Army 'Gunship' for day and night all-weather escort and attack missions. In advance of its time, the sheer magnitude of development problems and costs eventually resulted in its abandonment in 1969.*

continuing with the development of the advanced rigid rotor system. As a result of the 1969 cancellation for an AAFSS helicopter, the US Army decided its requirement for an Advanced Attack Helicopter (AAH) was important enough to warrant a new contest to find a successor for the Huey Cobra. In November 1972 therefore a design contest was launched for which the following five manufacturers submitted entries: Hughes, Bell, Boeing Vertol, Lockheed and Sikorsky. By June 1973, the competitors had been reduced from five to two and the survivors, Bell and Hughes Helicopters, were each awarded contracts to build two prototype aircraft and an engineering airframe for ground tests. The first Hughes prototype took to the air on 30 September 1975 at Palomar Airport, California; the Bell aircraft following it next day at Arlington, Texas. The fly-off competition between the two helicopters started in June 1976 and comprised 90 hours flying time during which the two types would be subjected to similar performance and handling tests.

At first glance the two helicopters are rather similar, but the Bell aircraft, the YAH-63A, was fitted with a two-bladed main rotor, a traditional feature of that manufacturer's helicopters, while the Hughes machine, the YAH-64A, employed a four-bladed system. Both were equipped with a wheeled undercarriage, the Bell with a tricycle nosewheel type, the Hughes with two mains and a tailwheel. The major difference between the two helicopters lay in the crew seating positions. In view of the Bell company's extensive gunship experience and from operating data taken from Huey and Huey Cobra missions in Vietnam, Bell's choice was to place the pilot in the front seat and the observer/gunner in the rear. In Bell's view, because of the increasingly accurate variety of low-level hostile weaponry liable to be ranged against future attack helicopters, the only method of operation that gave a good chance of survival was low-level or 'Nap of the Earth' (NOE) flying. Bell declared that the pilot, who will be operating at low level and often below the tree line, navigating and firing the on-board weapon systems, needs to be seated in front where he will have the best possible field of view.

Hughes, however, stuck with current practice and put their pilot's position at the rear and the co-pilot/gunner in the front. With their experience of NOE operations with the OH-6A Cayuse on scouting missions in Vietnam, Hughes concentrated their efforts into reducing all-up weight and increasing manoeuvrability. This policy paid off for Hughes when in December 1976, the YAH-64A was declared the winner of the AAH competition. Intended to take over the anti-tank role in the US Army from the Bell Huey Cobra, the AH-64A Apache is equipped with a wide range of advanced weapons and sensors. The initial requirement was for the AH-64A Apache to be armed with Hughes TOW missiles. Since its main mission will be to stand-off at a distance unseen by the enemy and kill tanks, the projected weapon fit was changed to that of the Rockwell International Hellfire system. This weapon, of which the Apache can carry eight mounted in two pods of four on its small stub wings, homes on to laser light diffused or reflected from its target. Secondary armament is the 30-mm Hughes Chain Gun and/or up to 76 70-mm free flight rockets.

Among the advanced equipment carried on this formidable helicopter are Black

Above *The anti-tank version of the SA 365 Dauphin 2 fitted with 'Venus' FLIR equipment and eight Euromissile 'HOT' missiles.*

Below *The AS 350L Ecureuil is a single-engined military machine which although used in the liasion and observation roles, can be armed with 20-mm cannon and rockets.*

Hole engine exhaust suppressors in which the hot gases from the powerplant are mixed with cold air before being expelled, thus denying infra-red heat seeking missiles a target to lock on to. The Target Acquisition and Designation System and Pilot's Night Vision Sensor (TADS/PNVS) provide the helicopter crew with the capability to detect, recognize and engage enemy targets at extended stand-off ranges during day, night and/or adverse weather conditions. The initial AAH design specification also called for the helicopter to be immune to rifle-calibre ammunition, with further immunity against occasional hits from weapons up to 12.7-mm calibre and for an ability to remain airborne after hits in critical parts with 23-mm weapons for thirty minutes.

The production version of the Apache helicopter is ballistically tolerant to armour piercing and high explosive incendiary rounds and during testing has demonstrated the capability to operate for five hours after taking a direct hit from a high explosive incendiary (HEI) round through a main rotor blade. This capability exceeds by ten times the US Army's specified requirement. As this potent tank killer is now entering squadron service, its advanced capabilities should help redress the present imbalance between the Warsaw Pact Forces and those of the NATO countries, hopefully deterring at the same time the expansionist tendencies of the Soviets.

In Great Britain the Westland Helicopter Company is also developing an improved anti-tank helicopter known as the Lynx 3. Evolved from the Team Lynx series, Lynx 3 shares the advantages of commonality of proven dynamic systems from the Team Lynx thus providing economic operation, training and

The twin-engined MBB BO 105 is in service with the armies of West Germany, Spain and the Netherlands as a light observation and anti-armour helicopter.

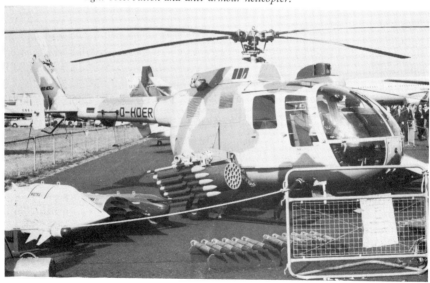

The Lynx 3 is a design for a combat support helicopter and the aircraft in this photograph is seen equipped with Rockwell Hellfire missiles, a mast-mounted sight, a wire strike protection system, TADS/PNVS and signature suppression equipment.

maintenance costs. Basically an improved version of the battlefield Lynx AH Mk 1, the series 3 is fitted with a wheeled tricycle undercarriage, is tolerant of ballistic damage and fitted with a crash-resistant fuel system. Like the Hughes AH-64A Apache, the Lynx 3 can be fitted with some very advanced weapons and sensors. Effective firepower is provided by Rockwell Hellfire, Euromissile HOT or Hughes TOW anti-armour missiles. Compatible with these weapon fits are the Martin Marietta TADS/PNVS.

Target acquisition systems can be mast or nose mounted and Lynx 3 can also be equipped with signature suppression and counter measures equipment in the form of IFF (Identification Friend or Foe) transponders, radar warning and jammers, infra-red receivers and chaff dispensers. For air-to-air defence General Dynamics Stinger missiles will be included in the Lynx 3 weapons pack. Powered by twin Rolls-Royce Gem 60 turboshaft engines and with a cruising speed of over 140 knots, the Lynx 3 will make a deadly addition to the tank-busting capability of any service should it ever decide to re-equip with the type. With much development of advanced attack helicopters being undertaken in the West, it must be remembered that across the Iron Curtain, the Soviet Union is also developing its own rival assault and armed attack helicopters. Standard attack helicopter with the Soviet Frontal Aviation Assault Units is the Mi-24 Hind, armed with a 12.7 mm manually-aimed machine gun in the nose and bearing six rocket pods containing 192 missiles, carried on two external stores racks.

Powered by twin Isotov 2,200 shp TV3-117 turboshafts with a maximum cruising speed of around 170 mph (275 km/h) the Hind is still in production, with a growing proportion of the aircraft being delivered to Soviet client states. The helicopter is currently on active service in Afghanistan where the type has proved effective against the Mujahideen guerrillas. Hinds operating in Afghanistan usually fly at fairly high level, their favourite tactics seem to involve diving head on attack to blast villages or guerrilla groups. Most examples of the Hind have large stub wings and multiple weapon and sensor fits. What appear to be optical and television heads may in fact be low light level and laser target rangers possibly allowing the gun and rocket pods to be operated effectively in poor light

The P-227 was a proposed joint Westland/VFW-Fokker design for an anti-tank attack helicopter for central European use in the late 1980s.

Above *The Mil Mi 8 is a Soviet general-purpose assault transport, armed gunship and civil commercial helicopter powered by twin Isotov turboshaft engines. This example has had its main rotor blades removed for transport by sea.*

Below *An Army Lynx fitted with the Bofors RBS 70 helicopter self defence system.*

conditions and/or at night. Externally visible aerials indicate the Hind carries
Doppler radar, a radio altimeter and VHF and HF radios. It is a large helicopter
with an overall estimated gross weight of 22,000 lb, a fuselage length of 55 ft 9 in
(17.0 m), a height of 14 ft (4.25 m) and a main rotor diameter of 55 ft 9 in (17.0 m).

The sheer size of the Hind ensures that it is much more easily detectable, both
in flight and on the ground, than any comparable Western attack helicopter. To
solve this problem of size, a new Soviet combat helicopter the Mi-28 Havoc is
under development. The Havoc is believed to more closely resemble the
American Hughes AH-64A Apache, but is again larger and is more probably like
the Lockheed AH-56 Cheyenne. This suggests that the Havoc could be designed
as an air-to-ground/air-to-air combat partner for the Mi-24 Hind, with much
improved agility thanks to its much smaller cross section, the Mi-28 having no
troop transport cabin. Little is known of this aircraft as yet although it is believed
to share the same Isotov powerplants as the Hind, but not the same main rotor
system. The type is expected to enter operational front line service sometime in the
late 1980s.

Battlefield transports

Perhaps more than any other of its many and varied roles the helicopter has really
come into its own as a battlefield transport. In military campaigns of the past,
assaults on land targets were usually accomplished either by direct frontal or flank
assault by infantry or armour or by dropping paratroops over the battle area. On
some occasions however, because of the difficulty of the terrain, both of these
methods are well nigh impossible. It is then that tactical assault helicopters really
prove their worth. One of the earlier conflicts where transport helicopters played a
significant part was the Six Day War between Israel and the Arab States in 1967.

In the Syrian-held Golan Heights fierce resistance was being met by the
advancing Israeli troops. The Syrian artillery positions on top of these hills could
only be reached by air—attempting an assault up the hillsides would have been
'suicide'. The Israelis therefore airlifted troops and artillery in Aérospatiale SA
321 Super Frelon helicopters directly to a spot at the rear of the enemy positions
and then successfully attacked and destroyed the Syrian camp. Ideal for this role,
the Super Frelon is a large three-engined utility transport helicopter powered by
Turbomeca Turmo 1,630 shp turboshafts. The largest and heaviest helicopter yet
built in quantity to a Western European design, the Super Frelon took to the air
on 7 December 1962 at Marignane in Southern France. All combat versions of the
Super Frelon can operate from land, ships or water and the type is in service with
the air arms of France, Libya, Syria, Iran and South Africa as well as Israel.

Aérospatiale also produce another battlefield transport (in collaboration with
Westland Helicopters) the SA 330 Puma, an aircraft designed in the early 1960s to
meet a requirement for a modern helicopter with a large unobstructed cabin,
equipped for all weather flying by day or night for the ALAT (French Army Light
Aviation). It was intended to replace the ageing piston-engined Sikorsky S-58 and
Vertol H-21. The first of two prototype aircraft took to the air on 15 April 1965
and six pre-production helicopters were built. All of these aircraft were flying by

The tandem-rotor CH-47D Chinook is the US Army's standard medium lift helicopter and is shown here during an operational exercise with US Airborne soldiers.

the summer of 1968 and the first production Puma made its maiden flight in September of that year. The SA 330 was selected by the British Royal Air Force as its standard tactical transport helicopter and it thus became one of the machines (along with the SA 341 Gazelle and the Westland WG 13 Lynx) to be built under a joint Anglo-French co-production agreement.

A medium sized transport helicopter the Puma is powered by twin Turbomeca Turmo 1,328 shp turboshafts which drive a main rotor of 49 ft 2½ in (15.0 m) giving a range of 355 miles (572 km), a maximum cruising speed of 168 mph (271 km/h), with accommodation for a crew of two and 16-20 fully-are armed troops or six stretchers and six seated patients. The aircraft that serve with the Royal Air Force are designated the SA 330E Puma HC Mk 1 and first flew on 25 November 1970. No 33 Squadron became the first RAF unit to form on the type in 1971, followed by No 230 Squadron in 1972. These squadrons operate the Puma in close support of the British Army from bases as far apart as Belize and Northern Ireland. In 1977, No 33 Squadron took over the United Kingdom commitment for NATO's ACE mobile force and takes part in many exercises stretching from Norway down to the Mediterranean coast. A further eight aircraft on top of the initial production batch were built for the RAF with the last example being delivered in 1981. The first French Army unit to operate the type became operational on the Puma in June 1970. Over 700 Pumas have been constructed, mostly for military customers but including many for civil operators. Though normally employed as an all-weather battlefield transport, Pumas can be fitted with a wide variety of weapons including machine guns, cannon, rockets and missiles. Overseas operators of the Puma include Abu Dhabi, Algeria, Belgium, Brazil, Chile, Ethiopia, Indonesia, Kenya, Mexico, Morocco, Nigeria, Portugal, Qatar, South Africa, Tunisia and Zaire. A variant of the Puma range, the AS 332 Super Puma, first flew on 13 September 1978. The Super Puma is superficially similar to the original aircraft, but is, in many respects, a very different machine. Apart from newer and more powerful engines, the AS 332 has a longer fuselage section, a more efficient glass-fibre composite main rotor, a revised landing gear and full de-icing.

After its experience with the Army Lynx, Westland have also developed independently their own multi-role transport helicopter, the Westland 30, a medium-weight assault transport which marries proven Team Lynx powerplants, transmission and rotor technology with a new high capacity cabin and fuselage. A natural development of the Lynx series, the helicopter first flew on 10 April 1979 and powered by twin Rolls-Royce 1,120 shp Gem 41-1 free turbine turboshafts with full IFR (Instrument Flight Rules) capability, it has the following specifications: an empty basic weight of 6,680 lb (3,030 kg), a maximum loaded weight of 12,000 lb (5,443 kg), a maximum cruising speed of 150 mph (241 km/h) and a radius of support action of 167 miles (269 km), a ferry range of 403 miles (648 km) and a payload range of 142 miles (228 km) with a 4,000 lb (1,814 kg) load. The Westland 30 can lift up to 22 soldiers with personnel weapons, awkward loads of internal or external cargo up to 5,000 lb (2,270 kg) and, in a casevac role, a load of six stretchers plus ten sitting patients and their attendants. Demonstrations and trials with a prototype Westland 30 in military configuration, took place in the summer of 1980 at the UK School of Infantry.

Until any orders are forthcoming for a replacement, the RAF's Pumas will continue to be partnered in the medium transport role by the Westland Wessex, a licence-built version of the Sikorsky S-58. Westland acquired the licence production rights for the Sikorsky S-58 from the parent company in 1956. Before setting production in the United Kingdom however, they imported a Sikorsky built S-58 in HSS-1 configuration. This aircraft was subsequently test flown with its original Wright R-1820-84 1,525 hp piston engine and was then modified to take the Napier Gazelle NGA 11-1,100 shp turboshaft engine and in this form it took to the air on 17 May 1957. This prototype was joined by two pre-production Wessex HAS Mk 1s for pre-service naval trials. The Wessex was soon adopted by the Royal Navy as a cheaper and more reliable replacement for the Bristol 191 tandem rotor helicopter. Upon the successful conclusion of trials, deliveries of production Wessex HAS Mk 1s commenced in 1960. In 1962 HMS *Albion*, a commando carrier, received the Wessex Mk 1 in a sixteen-seat assault transport version. Meanwhile, the Royal Air Force purchased a twin-engined version designated the Wessex HC Mk 2, powered by twin Bristol Siddeley Gnome turboshafts. The first production version of this aircraft made its maiden flight on 5 October 1962. In all the Royal Air Force received some 72 HC Mk 2s which are used extensively for search and rescue, training, troop carrying and transport duties. Serving with various squadrons in the UK and overseas, notably Hong Kong, the type is no longer considered a modern battlefield transport. Two of the

Above *The AS 332 Super Puma tactical transport helicopter deploys a 'stick' of French troops.*

Below *Standard battlefield transport helicopter of the RAF, which operates the type with 33 and 230 Squadrons, and the French ALAT is the Westland/Aerospatiale Puma.*

Air Force machines were converted from HC Mk 2 standard into HCC Mk 4 VIP transports to serve with the Queen's Flight. The Wessex has proved to be one of Westland's most successful and enduring aircraft.

The Royal Navy's successor to the Wessex is the Westland Commando, a land-based variant of the Sea King intended mainly for troop or freight transport, logistic support and casualty evacuation. With power supplied by twin Rolls-Royce Gnome 1,500 shp H-1400-1 turboshafts, the Commando can lift up to 28 fully-armed troops and carry a crew of three. Provision for a variety of guns and weapons is made thus equipping the Commando for the support role. Originally announced in 1971, the Commando Mk 1 was ordered by Saudi Arabia on the behalf of Egypt and first flew in September 1973, with deliveries following in the months of January and February 1974. As the initial and most basic conversion of the Sea King, the Mk 1 could only lift some 21 equipped troops. The production and more specialized version, the Commando Mk 2, first flew on 16 January 1975. This has a fixed undercarriage and other changes and nineteen Mk 2Bs were ordered for the Egyptian Air Force, including two as VIP Mk 2B transports. Other users include the Royal Navy's Fleet Air Arm, where the type is known as the Sea King HC 4 and was operated to great effect in the Falklands Campaign. Other overseas customers include the Qatar Air Force which operates three Commando Mk 2A troop transports and one Mk 2C VIP transport.

A Westland Whirlwind Mk 10 of RAF Transport Command.

Above *This Westland 30 multi-role battlefield helicopter lifts off over the mortar team it has just deployed during tactical flying trials.*

Below *Westland Whirlwind 3 in Brunei markings, with a civil Wessex in the background.*

Above *This Mk 52 version of the Westland Wessex served with the armed forces of Iraq.*

Below *In this rather dated picture a Royal Air Force Wessex Mk 2 of Transport Command embarks a 'stick' of infantry soldiers during an exercise.*

Above *This Westland Wessex Mk 4 serves on VIP duties with the Queen's Flight.*

Below *Westland Commando helicopters of the Qatar Emiri Air Force. These machines serve on VIP duties.*

Above *An Egyptian Air Force Commando VIP Mk 2B helicopter.*

Below *Providing support for commando, amphibious assault and landing operations, Westland Sea King HC 4 helicopters can carry underslung external loads of up to 8,000 lb (3,600 kg) or a variety of internal cargos including up to 28 fully-armed troops.*

American developments

With the largest armed forces in the Western World, the American military services are major operators of battlefield transport helicopters. The primary helicopter operator in the United States is the US Army with over 9,000 machines, including a huge fleet of Huey transports, one of the best known of all helicopters and certainly one of the most prolific considering that the type has been in almost constant production in one form or another for over twenty years.

In June 1955, the prototype Huey (XH-40) won a US Army design competition for a new utility, training and casevac helicopter. The XH-40 first flew on 22 October 1956, and following this flight, construction of a further six aircraft was authorized for pre-service trials, the only changes from the prototype being uprated engine power, the fitting of landing skids and a larger main cabin. After successful testing of these aircraft, the US Army received the first of nine pre-production machines for field evaluation in June 1959. Concluding this evaluation the first 74 aircraft of the initial production batch, designated HU-1 Iroquois, were delivered to the Army. The HU designation was changed in 1962 to UH and it was these letters than originated the nickname 'Huey' which has stuck with the aircraft to the present day. With the United States drawn into the Vietnam conflict the Huey really came into its own in South-East Asia and was to that operation what the 'jeep' was to World War 2. In Vietnam, the UH-1B went into action with M-60 machine guns and free flight rockets as outlined in the section on gunship development. In 1965 while Bell were developing a dedicated attack helicopter to take over the role that the UH-1B had pioneered, the UH-1C came into service to replace the B version in 1965 and was a great improvement with increased speed and manoeuvrability. Preceding the UH-1C in 1963, however, was the UH-1D which was the most numerous development of the type with over a thousand examples being built. The real workhorse of the Huey series, the UH-1D was the main battlefield support helicopter in Vietnam, as well as flying on just about every other conceivable type of mission from casualty evacuations to gunship, spares truck and garbage hauler.

The US Air Force purchased 146 models of the UH-1F version for missile support duties. First flight of the UH-1F version was on 20 February 1964 and deliveries began to the USAF in September the same year. The principal version for the United States Marine Corps is the twin-engined UH-1N. For the US Army, no UH-1G version was announced and instead the series jumped to the UH-1H and over 600 of these models were ordered to replace or supplement the UH-1D. Huey helicopters have been supplied to civil and military operators all over the world. The type was manufactured under licence by Agusta in Italy, Dornier in West Germany and Fuji in Japan. Among the overseas customers for the Huey are Austria, Greece, Iran, Oman, Morocco, Spain, Sweden, Turkey, Kuwait and Norway. On 30 August 1972, the US Department of Defense announced that a competition to build a helicopter to replace the Huey as the US Army's standard battlefield assault aircraft would take place between Sikorsky and Boeing Vertol. The Army's Utility Tactical Transport Aircraft System (UTTAS) requirement called for three prototype aircraft from each manufacturer, the winner being announced after a series of trials and engineering tests. The two competing helicopters were the Sikorsky YUH-60A and the Boeing Vertol YUH-61A.

The first YUH-60A took to the air on 17 October 1974 and the remaining two prototypes of the same aircraft were also flying by February 1975. After an intensive seven-month-long fly-off against the YUH-61A, the Sikorsky design was pronounced the winner on 23 December 1976. Production was initiated in the autumn of 1977 with deliveries from the first batch due in August 1978. Designated the UH-60 Blackhawk and powered by twin General Electric 1,543 shp T700-GE-700 turbines, the Blackhawk cruises at 184 mph (296 km/h). The entire helicopter airframe is designated to withstand fire from 7.62-mm bullets and the main rotor blades can survive strikes from 23-mm shells. Design features include a low profile shape and this enables one to be lifted in a Lockheed C-130 Hercules or six in a Lockheed C-5A Galaxy. Operated by a crew of three the Blackhawk can carry eleven fully-equipped troops or four stretchers. Armament can be one or two machine guns firing through side doors—there are no plans to make this helicopter into a gunship, that role being reserved for the Hughes AH-64A Apache. Approximately 1,107 Blackhawks are being delivered to the US Army and the type has already seen action, being used in the American invasion of Grenada in October 1983. The type is also expected to serve with the US Air Force on various duties.

The Sikorsky H-37A Mojave was the US Army's standard heavy assault transport helicopter in the late 1950s.

Above *The Bell UH-1F serves with the United States Air Force on missile support duties.*

Below *The Sikorsky S-61R is known in US Air Force service as the HH-3E or 'Jolly Green Giant' and the type serves in the assault, troop transport and combat rescue roles.*

Above *The well-known Bell Huey series was the main American battlefield support helicopter in Vietnam, flying on every conceivable type of operation. This model is a UH-1H and this type among others served as a 'Dust off' (named after the radio call sign of Major Charles Kelly, a US helicopter pilot killed in action in 1964) casualty evacuation aircraft crewed by two pilots, a crewman and a medical aidman to give emergency medical treatment in the air.*

Below *The Sikorsky S-65 is known in US Air Force service as the HH-53C.*

Above *A fine air-to-air shot of a Blackhawk helicopter in cruising flight.*

Below *The Sikorsky UH-60 Blackhawk, although a relatively new helicopter, has already seen action with the US Army, the type being used in the American invasion of Granada in October 1983.*

Above *Replacing the Bell UH-1 Huey as the standard US Army utility helicopter is the Sikorsky Blackhawk, seen here lifting a field artillery weapon.*

Below *The Boeing Vertol YUH-61A was the unsuccessful rival to the Sikorsky YUH-60 Blackhawk in the US Army's UTTAS competition.*

Soviet big lifters

The Soviet Union did not take long to develop and produce transport helicopters and from the earliest days its machines have been large and powerful. One of the earliest Soviet assault transports was the Mil Mi 6 Hook, the standard Warsaw Pact heavy transport helicopter, which first flew in 1957. For more than ten years after its unveiling it remained the largest helicopter in the world and was also the first Soviet turbine-powered machine to enter series production. Five prototype aircraft were built, the first of these flying in the autumn of 1957. During its subsequent flight test programme, the Mi 6 established a number of world records for speed and payload before entering service, it is believed, in early 1960. Powered by twin 5,500 shp Soloviev D-25VTV-2BM turbines, it has a main rotor diameter of 114 ft 10 in (35.0 m), a fuselage length of 108 ft 10½ in (33.18 m), a height of 32 ft 4 in (9.86 m), an empty weight of 60,000 lb (27,240 kg), a maximum gross weight of 93,700 lb (42,500 kg) and a maximum speed of 186 mph (300 km/h).

Over 800 of these impressive helicopters have been built with nearly all thought to have been delivered to the military. These huge machines have been observed in several major field exercises, where payloads have included up to 68 fully-equipped troops or military vehicles in underslung loads. Operated by a crew of five the Hook can lift 26,450 lb (12,000 kg) of internal cargo, 19,840 lb (9,000 kg) of externally slung cargo or, in a casevac role, 41 stretchers plus two attendants. The

The Mil Mi 6 is a heavy transport and flying crane helicopter in service with the Soviet armed forces and with the civil operator Aeroflot. It is fitted with clamshell rear doors (seen here open) for the loading of passengers and freight and has shoulder level small fixed wings to relieve the load on the main rotor during flight.

This massive four-engined, lateral rotor Mil Mi 12 is more like a fixed-wing airliner than a helicopter. Operated by a six-man crew the Mil Mi 12 can lift loads compatible with the giant Anatov AN-22 transport aircraft. The type is in service with the state airline Aeroflot as well as with the Soviet armed forces.

aircraft is also fitted with large rear clamshell doors and folding ramps which offer easy loading of vehicles and freight.

Operated by many of the Soviet satellite states, others have also been supplied to Egypt, Peru, Syria, Indonesia, Algeria, Ethiopia, Libya and Afghanistan. Larger even than the Mi 6 is the Mil Mi 10, a heavy lift flying crane development of the Mi 6 and known in the West by its NATO code name Harke. First seen at Tushino in 1961, the Mi 10 employs the proven main rotor system and powerplants of the Mi 6 but does not have that aircraft's stub wings for rotor offloading. Available in a tall or short-legged version and normally operated by a crew of three, up to 28 troops and/or freight can be carried in the main cabin, but the primary cargo is lifted externally. On the long-legged version, cargoes, particularly vehicles, can be pre-loaded on specially designed wheeled platforms and locked into position between the undercarriage. Alternatively the helicopter can be taxied into position over the load, which is then attached to the landing gear at special fixing points. The Mil Mi 10 is thought to be in service with units of the Soviet armed forces in probably much the same role as the US Army Reserve's S-64 Skycrane.

Chapter 3

Helicopters at sea

The naval helicopter is today accepted as an integral part of a ship's weapon system, as important as the gun turret or the missile launcher. The versatility of the helicopter is one of its most valuable attributes, being able to go to sea and operate aboard almost any size of surface warship in pursuit of a number of objectives. These objectives take many forms and although the main task of the naval helicopter is anti-submarine warfare it may also be called on to perform surface search, surface strike, radar control, reconnaissance, flare drop, transfer of personnel, torpedo drop, casualty evacuation and stores replenishment. Much of the early work with helicopters, particularly helicopters of wartime German design, was with naval variants of the machine.

The FL 265 and FL 282 Kolibri were the first true helicopters to enter naval service, the FL 282 along with the Sikorsky R4, even seeing limited operational service at the tail end of the Second World War. By the end of the early post-war years, it was apparent that the helicopter was here to stay and the Royal Navy's Fleet Air Arm began to think of ways to get the helicopter to sea. The helicopter at this time was rather crude and underdeveloped and operating them in the anti-submarine role at sea was for the moment impossible. Numerous trials with the R4 were conducted, the first of these being on a North Atlantic convoy in 1944.

That year a fifty-ship convoy left New York bound for England and among its vessels was the SS *Daghestan* with two Sikorsky R4s aboard. Four test pilots were included in the ship's company for this trial, one Royal Navy pilot, one US Coast Guard pilot and two pilots from the Royal Air Force. Unfortunately, because of rough weather the trial was unsuccessful and very little flying was accomplished, although one of the pilots did manage one flight in mid-Atlantic. Although this particular trial had been a failure, the future potential of the helicopter was plain for all to see and the Royal Navy recommended that further development should continue. A large number of R4 or Hoverflies, as they were known in British service, had been ordered by the Royal Navy under lend-lease arrangements, but only 45 machines had been delivered by the end of hostilities. The Hoverfly although disappointing as a potential anti-submarine warfare machine did have potential as an air-sea rescue aircraft and the Royal Navy wasted no time in utilizing the aircraft for this purpose.

It was decided to centralize all available helicopter knowledge into a trials unit and 771 Squadron was formed in September 1945, this unit becoming the first to receive the Hoverfly in quantity. Becoming operational at Portland, Dorset, in the same month, 771 flew as a Fleet Requirements Unit on general duties, but continued with the development of air-sea rescue techniques. In 1946 Westland obtained a licence from Sikorsky to manufacture the S-51 in Great Britain and so began a long association between the two manufacturers which continues to this day. Until Westland could begin to manufacture and deliver the S-51 in numbers, the Fleet Air Arm would continue to amass operating data for future use with its Hoverflies. A second sea-borne trial was arranged with the Hoverfly, and an R4 piloted by one Lieutenant Alan Bristow (who would later build up one of the world's largest commercial helicopter companies) was flown on to HMS *Helmsdale* for trials. Like the earlier trials these were not a great success but it was obvious that as soon as performance and payload could be increased here would be the makings of a fine anti-submarine warfare (ASW) vehicle.

In the meantime, the ageing Sea Otter air-sea rescue aircraft was due to be replaced and Westland developed the S-51 Dragonfly to meet that requirement. Thus the first operational role of the Royal Navy's helicopters was air-sea rescue. It was envisaged that as a result of this decision there would be an increase in the number of helicopter pilots needed to fly these new machines and the first all-helicopter unit, No 705 Squadron, was formed at RNAS Gosport on 7 May 1947. Equipped with Hoverfly R4B aircraft and later the R6, 705 Squadron operated on

An R-4 Hoverfly helicopter with floats operating from Portland harbour.

Above *This naval version of the AS 332F Super Puma is carrying two AM 39 Exocet missiles.*

Below *An Aérospatiale SA 321G Super Frelon fires an AM 39 Exocet missile during the latter's development programme.*

radar alignment and communications duties in addition to its training role. During this time, the first landing by a Fleet Air Arm helicopter on a ship at sea was carried out when a Hoverfly was recovered to the foredeck of the battleship HMS *Vanguard* off Portland, whilst the ship was en-route to South Africa with the Royal Family aboard.

The development of the Dragonfly soon ran into problems and in the interim period, 705 Squadron received a number of Sikorsky R6 Hoverfly 2 aircraft. This refined and developed version of the R4 did not enjoy a long service career and after being beset by engine problems was finally withdrawn in 1950. The first Dragonfly took to the air on 5 October 1948 and the first Royal Navy Dragonfly, the HR Mk 1 version, flew on 22 June 1949—these aircraft entering service with 705 Squadron in 1950.

Notable among many resuce operations in which the Dragonfly took part, was the much publicized *Flying Enterprise* rescue. On 10 January 1952, the American freighter *Flying Enterprise* was adrift in the South-West Approaches, listing badly and fighting a 50-knot gale in an attempt to make port. Only two crew remained on board the ship which was near to capsizing. Two Dragonfly helicopters from 705 Squadron set out to reach her and rescue the crew who had been observed struggling for a hold on the funnel. One of the aircraft ran into trouble and had to land to refuel at Exeter. The other landed at RNAS Culdrose, Cornwall, to refuel before setting out into the gale. The pilot managed to fly his helicopter to within 30 miles of the stricken freighter's position, but the headwind and extreme turbulence reduced his ground speed so much that he too was eventually forced to turn back. Happily the Captain and First Mate on the *Flying Enterprise* did not perish but were picked up a few hours later by another ship, the *Turmoil*. Although the air-sea rescue attempt itself had been unsuccessful, the operation's significance lies in the fact that the helicopter had been manually flown throughout the whole operation, no auto-stabilizing devices or other pilot aids being available at the time. Dragonflies served not only with 705 Squadron but

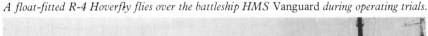

A float-fitted R-4 Hoverfly flies over the battleship HMS Vanguard *during operating trials.*

also with 701, 727, 728 and 771 Squadrons. The last Dragonfly helicopter in Royal Navy service was withdrawn from use with Britannia Flight at the Royal Naval College Dartmouth in June 1967, thus ending seventeen years of continuous service.

Above *Three early types of Fleet Air Arm helicopter fly in formation—the Sikorsky S-51, R-6 and R-4B (top to bottom).*

Below *A novel way of taking a NAFFI break.*

Above *A 705 Squadron Hiller 12E at RNAS Culdrose. The type was in service as the Royal Navy's basic helicopter trainer for over twenty years before being replaced by the Westland Gazelle.*

Below *Replacing the Hiller 12E as the Fleet Air Arm's basic rotary wing trainer in service with 705 Squadron at RNAS Culdrose, is the Gazelle HT Mk 2.*

War against the submarine

Whilst the Dragonfly had been gathering data on rescue operations and training helicopter pilots, the next generation of Royal Navy helicopters was preparing to enter service. The Whirlwind was a version of the S-55 built by Westland under licence from Sikorsky. The Fleet Air Arm received ten Sikorsky-built S-55s designated HRS-2s and fifteen HO4S-3s and these were known in British naval service as the HAR Mk 21 and HAR Mk 22 respectively, being used for rescue and anti-submarine duties. The first Whirlwind constructed by Westland flew on 12 November 1952 and the first Royal Naval unit to become operational on the type was 848 Squadron, which commissioned in the same year and whose service with the type in Malaya has been covered earlier.

The Whirlwind was a larger aircraft than the Dragonfly, having a main rotor diameter of 49 ft (14.94 m), a fuselage length of 42 ft 2 in (12.85 m) and a height of 13 ft 4 in (4.06 m). Powered by a 600 hp Pratt & Whitney engine (later replaced with a 750 hp Alvis Leonides piston engine), the Whirlwind offered a maximum speed of 105 mph (169 km/h), a service ceiling of 12,900 ft (3,392 m) and a typical operating range of 440 miles (708 km). Various progressively improved Whirlwinds entered service with the Navy: the Whirlwind Mk 3, powered by the 700 hp Wright R-1300-3 Wasp engine came into service in 1955, the first British aircraft carrier to operate this variant being HMS *Ark Royal*.

At this time the anti-submarine performance of the Whirlwind was rather embarrassing, its lack of endurance and limited weapon carrying ability were significant problems. The answer to these limitations came along on 17 October 1956 when the improved Whirlwind Mk 7 took to the air. After pre-service trials with 700 Squadron, the Intensive Flying Trials Unit (IFTU) at RNAS Lee-on-Solent, the Mk 7 entered Fleet Air Arm service in June 1957 with 845 Squadron. The Whirlwind Mk 7 was still not an adequate vehicle for the demanding anti-submarine warfare role as it could carry either the weapons or the sonar but not both! The Mk 7 continued in operational service, however: indeed the Whirlwind was not finally withdrawn from use until 1975 when the Gazelle replaced the type as a training aircraft.

Between 1959 and 1960, Westland converted a piston-engined Whirlwind to take a 1,050 shp Gnome turboshaft engine. This new version of the Whirlwind was known as the Mk 9 and it offered an impressive increase in reliability and performance over the piston-engined Mk 7, although the only external difference between the two aircraft was the lengthened nose of the Mk 9. A number of surplus Navy Mk 7s were converted to Mk 9 standard and these were mainly used in the search and rescue role, although two aircraft did go to sea aboard HMS *Protector* and, later, HMS *Endurance*. The Whirlwind was never the ideal aircraft for any of its many and varied roles but it paved the way for the third generation of naval helicopters.

Advances in sonar detecting equipment now required even larger and more powerful aircraft to take the system to sea. The successor to the Whirlwind in Fleet Air Arm service was the Westland Wessex, a licence-built version of the Sikorsky S-58. The Sikorsky S-58 had been designed to meet a US Navy requirement for a replacement for the Bell HSL-1, and entered US Naval service in late 1955. The S-58 introduced a number of advanced systems including day and night instrumentation, auto-pilot and the hover coupler. This latter device enabled the helicopter to hover whilst dunking the sonar by day or night. It is not always possible to hover a helicopter accurately at night when flown manually because of the lack of visual references, particularly when operating over water. American experience with the HSS-1 had shown the aircraft to be ineffective in the anti-submarine search and strike role and initially the helicopter was operated in pairs, one performing the hunter role, the other the killer. (The HSS-1 did, however, do a good job on search missions, where its superior speed and operating flexibility gave it an edge over corvettes and anti-submarine destroyers.)

A significant advance in anti-submarine technology was the development of the dipping sonar. Helicopters such as the Bell HSL-1 had carried large numbers of bulky expendable sonabuoys, which were rather low powered and dropped one after another in search of the enemy vessel. With just one large and powerful sonar which could be repeatedly dipped into position and then moved to a different place, the anti-submarine helicopter really became the eyes and ears of the parent ship. When Westland acquired a licence to manufacture the Wessex system in Britain in 1956 a great deal of the development work had already been done. The most significant alteration of the basic S-58 undertaken by Westland was the re-engining of the aircraft with a turboshaft powerplant. The original Wright R-

This SA 321G Super Frelon winches up a frogman/diver after a simulated rescue/recovery exercise.

Above *This Westland Whirlwind HAS Mk 7 was the final version of the Whirlwind to serve with the Fleet Air Arm, although some seventeen aircraft were later converted to Mk 9 standard.*
Below *A Whirlwind 3 of the Brazilian Navy.*

1820-84 1,525 hp piston engine was replaced with a Napier Gazelle NGA-11 1,100 shp turbine and this new form flew on 17 May 1957. Two more pre-production aircraft completed for naval trials were known as Wessex HAS Mk 1s.

The Mk 1 was operated by a crew of four (pilot, co-pilot, observer and sonar operator) and came into operational service in July 1961. A number of squadrons were equipped with the type, including 848 Squadron on commando assault duties aboard HMS *Albion*. The ASW gear could be removed from their aircraft to make room for sixteen fully equipped troops or eight stretchers plus one attendant if used in a casualty evacuation role. Eventually the main anti-submarine version of the Wessex in Royal Navy service became the Mk 3. This entered service in January 1967 and was distinguishable from the earlier Mk 1 by the large dorsal radome, which resulted in the aircraft acquiring the popular nickname of 'Camel'. The Camel was fitted with a more powerful engine than the Mk 1, a 1,600 shp Mk 165 Gazelle and at last provided the complete anti-submarine deterrent, being fitted with a new British-constructed long-range sonar, a more powerful radar and a much more substantial flight control system than that fitted to the Mk 1 aircraft. The only apparent drawback to this helicopter was that its operating range was less than the Whirlwind Mk 7. The Wessex Mk 3 mainly operated aboard the 'County' class destroyers of the Royal Navy and also with 737 Squadron which conducted advanced training for observers and sonar operators prior to sea service. In addition to its service with the Fleet Air Arm, the Wessex was also supplied to the Royal Australian Navy, which received 27 of the HAS Mk 31 version, powered by the Gazelle 162 1,540 shp turbine for a variety of duties. When the Wessex Mk 3 was introduced into the anti-submarine role, the Mk 1 was not retired but continued to serve with 771 Squadron, Royal Navy, on search and rescue duties based at RNAS Culdrose in Cornwall.

The Westland Wessex offered superior performance to the original Sikorsky design primarily as a result of the fitting of a turboshaft engine, which is both intrinsically more compact and lighter than piston powerplants. The turboshaft also uses safer fuel and is much more reliable. In America, the US Navy, after their initial experience with the Sikorsky HSS-1, needed a helicopter designed from the start to be fitted with turbine powerplants. The basis for such a design was already flying in the shape of the Sikorsky S-62. Originating in 1957-58, the S-62 used the same main and tail rotor, transmission and other systems of the earlier piston-engined S-55, the American equivalent of the Westland Whirlwind. The fuselage and powerplant of this machine, however, were entirely new: the S-62 boasted a flying-boat-type hull with stabilizing floats, a retractable undercarriage and a single 1,250 shp General Electrical GT-58-110-1 turboshaft engine. This engine was so small and light that it could be mounted above the cabin roof next to the main rotor gearbox, which resulted in a much roomier main cabin that could accommodate up to twelve people.

The S-62 first flew on 22 May 1958 and the type was the first turbine-powered American helicopter to be granted a type approval certificate by the Federal Aviation Administration (FAA). After pre-service trials in 1962 the US Navy ordered four of these machines, which, designated HU2S-1G, served with the US

The Sikorsky HSS-1N (later changed to SH-34) Seabat of the US Navy was employed from the late 1950s in the anti-submarine and utility roles.

Coast Guard. Subsequent USCG versions of the S-62 are known as the HH-52A and some 99 aircraft have entered service since early 1963.

The US Navy's anti-submarine requirement involved an enlarged version of the S-62 but with two engines in place of one. The prototype of this helicopter was known as the XHSS-2 and it took to the air on 11 March 1959. In the following year seven pre-production aircraft, now designated SH-3A Sea King, were evaluated in service trials before deliveries of production versions to the US Naval Air Squadrons began in September 1961. The Royal Navy discovered that the Sea King could operate from existing RN carriers and commando ships, including the two specialist helicopter cruisers HMS *Tiger* and HMS *Blake*. It was envisaged that the Sea King would take over the all-weather anti-submarine and search and rescue roles from the Wessex, thus providing a modern aircraft that would meet the Fleet Air Arm's requirements throughout the 1970s and 1980s. In 1967, Westland acquired licence production rights from Sikorsky to build the Sea King in Great Britain. An initial Royal Navy order for sixty aircraft was announced and these machines were to be powered by British engines and fitted with British electronics.

Westland's first production Sea King helicopter left *terra firma* on 7 May 1969, and the Sea King Intensive Flying Trials Unit was formed at RNAS Culdrose, tasked with evaluating the aircraft prior to service entry. During these trials the aircraft's performance was outstanding and the helicopter was rated as the Royal Navy's most potent anti-submarine aircraft yet. That rating is still true today,

Royal Navy commando Wessex HU 5 run up their engines on the flight deck of the carrier HMS Albion.

sixteen years later. The first Royal Naval unit to operate the Sea King formed up at RNAS Culdrose on 24 February 1970 and was embarked on the aircraft carrier HMS *Ark Royal*. Unlike American ASW helicopters which operate as an extension of the parent warship, Fleet Air Arm Sea Kings operate totally independently. The Royal Navy's helicopters therefore are equipped with weapons, sensors and a tactical command position to track down and destroy submerged submarines without the assistance of the mother ship. The observer is responsible not only for navigating the helicopter but also for directing and controlling his own weapons and those of other ships and aircraft.

Powered by two Rolls-Royce Gnome 1,400-1,500 shp turbine engines, the latest British Sea King variant, the Mk 5, has equipment for all-weather ASW operations, including search radar, an advanced flight control system, radio altimeters, Doppler radar, dipping sonar, two or four Stingray torpedoes, four depth charges or other ASW weapons. The Sea King is as large an aircraft again as the Wessex was over the Whirlwind. It has a main rotor diameter of 62 ft (18.9 m), a height of 16 ft 10 in (5.13 m) and a fuselage length of 55 ft 10 in (17.2 m). The main rotor blades and tail cone of the Sea King can be folded hydraulically which is why the rotor hub of this helicopter is more complex than most. Over 300 Westland-built Sea Kings are in service with the Royal Navy and with overseas customers: Australia, Belgium, Pakistan, India, West Germany, Norway and Egypt.

The future replacement of the Sea King helicopter has already been decided in the form of the EH-101, a joint production venture by Westland of Great Britain

The Westland Wessex HU 5 in addition to being standard equipment with two training squadrons (Nos 772 and 707) also served with four front line squadrons, Nos 845, 846, 847 and 848, with the first of these embarking for sea duty in 1967 aboard the commando carrier HMS Bulwark.

and Agusta of Italy. The EH-101 began life as a British Ministry of Defence (Navy) design study in 1974 and was originally designated the Westland WG-34. The EH-101 will be slightly smaller than the present Sea King and a new Royal Navy frigate, the Type 23, is to have a specially designed platform to take this new helicopter to sea. Initial studies showed that as a Sea King replacement, the EH-101 would achieve the best results if it had a long range and endurance plus high operating performance. Sensor equipment is likely to include sonabuoys, radar, radar interception equipment and a magnetic anomaly detector (MAD). The latter enables a helicopter to locate a submerged submarine by detecting the minute disturbance it makes in the Earth's magnetic field.

The EH-101 will be much more powerful than the Sea King—power will be supplied via three Rolls-Royce/Turbomeca RTM-322 turbines or General Electric T700-CT-7 powerplants driving a five-bladed main rotor giving a maximum speed of 198 mph (318 km/h), a range of 1,265 miles (2,035 km) and an endurance on two engines of over nine hours. The EH-101 design was accepted in 1978 and participation by Agusta was announced in 1980. The initial crew requirement for ASW operations is three, these being pilot, observer and accoustic systems operator. Both Westland and Agusta will manufacture the EH-101. Armament is expected to include homing torpedoes, such as Stingray, and possibly air-to-surface missiles. In the commando transport role the EH-101 should provide accommodation for 32 fully-armed troops.

Above *The Wessex Mk 31 served with the Royal Australian Navy before being replaced with the Westland Sea King.*

Left *A Royal Navy Wessex 3 or 'Camel' dipping its sonar during an anti-submarine search.*

Below *This Sikorsky HH-52, the military version of the Sikorsky S-62 serves with the Japanese Maritime Self Defence Force.*

Above *The Sikorsky S-61 is known in US Navy service as the SH-3 Sea King. It is the standard US anti-submarine, transport and general-purpose helicopter.*

Left *This Sea King of 819 Naval Air Squadron based at Prestwick Airport in Scotland operates in support of the Royal Marines stationed at HMS Condor, Arbroath.*

Below *Diagram of the Westland Sea King cockpit area showing the location of the various control panels.*

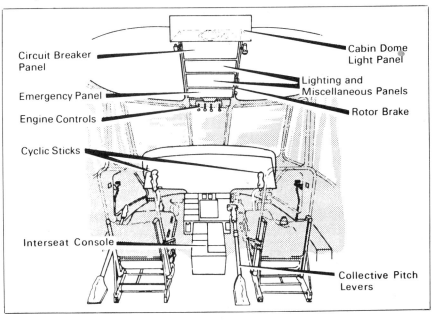

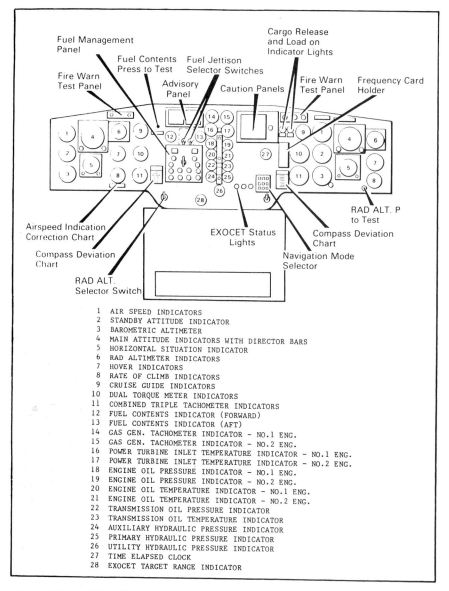

1   AIR SPEED INDICATORS
2   STANDBY ATTITUDE INDICATOR
3   BAROMETRIC ALTIMETER
4   MAIN ATTITUDE INDICATORS WITH DIRECTOR BARS
5   HORIZONTAL SITUATION INDICATOR
6   RAD ALTIMETER INDICATORS
7   HOVER INDICATORS
8   RATE OF CLIMB INDICATORS
9   CRUISE GUIDE INDICATORS
10 DUAL TORQUE METER INDICATORS
11 COMBINED TRIPLE TACHOMETER INDICATORS
12 FUEL CONTENTS INDICATOR (FORWARD)
13 FUEL CONTENTS INDICATOR (AFT)
14 GAS GEN. TACHOMETER INDICATOR - NO.1 ENG.
15 GAS GEN. TACHOMETER INDICATOR - NO.2 ENG.
16 POWER TURBINE INLET TEMPERATURE INDICATOR - NO.1 ENG.
17 POWER TURBINE INLET TEMPERATURE INDICATOR - NO.2 ENG.
18 ENGINE OIL PRESSURE INDICATOR - NO.1 ENG.
19 ENGINE OIL PRESSURE INDICATOR - NO.2 ENG.
20 ENGINE OIL TEMPERATURE INDICATOR - NO.1 ENG.
21 ENGINE OIL TEMPERATURE INDICATOR - NO.2 ENG.
22 TRANSMISSION OIL PRESSURE INDICATOR
23 TRANSMISSION OIL TEMPERATURE INDICATOR
24 AUXILIARY HYDRAULIC PRESSURE INDICATOR
25 PRIMARY HYDRAULIC PRESSURE INDICATOR
26 UTILITY HYDRAULIC PRESSURE INDICATOR
27 TIME ELAPSED CLOCK
28 EXOCET TARGET RANGE INDICATOR

Above *Westland Sea King instrument panel explanatory diagram.*

Top right *A Fleet Air Arm Sea King on the aft flight deck of the helicopter cruiser HMS* Tiger.

Right *The cockpit of the Westland Sea King.*

Above *This Sea King helicopter is in service with the Navy of Pakistan.*

Below *The complex rotor head of the Sea King which incorporates an automatic main rotor blade folding system to assist with stowage at sea.*

Above *A Royal Navy Westland Sea King Helicopter fitted with Thorn-EMI 'Search-Water' advanced marine early-warning radar. During the Falklands conflict this system was installed into aircraft in record time to fill the gap caused by the Fleet Air Arm's total lack of airborne early-warning radar.*

Below *Westland Sea King aircraft of the Egyptian Navy.*

Above *A Sea King of the Indian Navy.*

Below *A new Royal Navy frigate, the type 23 is to have a specially designed flight deck for a new naval helicopter, the Sea King replacement. The helicopter, the EH-101 is being built on a collaborative basis by Westland and Agusta to meet the needs of the navies of both nations.*

Small ships' helicopters

One of the most vital contributions of the helicopter to naval aviation has been the provision of small ships' Flights. From the Royal Navy's point of view, the Fleet Air Arm have always tried to have aircraft at sea in every available surface ship. Of course, the UK has not been alone in this ambition, for most of the world's navies have marine aviation arms and many operate helicopters from their surface vessels. One of the most compact small ships' helicopters, the Agusta A-106, was constructed to meet an Italian Navy requirement. It was a single-seat anti-submarine attack helicopter designed to serve aboard the *'Impavido'* class of guided missile destroyers.

Evolved from the earlier piston-engined series of A-103, A-104 and A-105, the prototype A-106 took to the air in November 1965. The A-106 was capable of operating in poor weather and equipment carried included two Mk 44 underslung homing torpedoes, target identification equipment, floatation gear and for shipboard stowage the main and tail rotors could be folded. If operated in the anti-surface vessel role, the torpedo armament was substituted for up to ten 80-mm free-flight rockets or two 7.62-mm machine guns. Following the aircraft's first flight, five pre-production machines were constructed for trials which, although successful, did not result in follow-on orders.

The United Kingdom's equivalent to the A-106 was the Westland Wasp. The Fleet Air Arm's Wasp helicopter evolved from the Saunders-Roe P 531 which was under development in the late 1950s as a general utility helicopter for the British Army. Many of the components used in the P 531 were the same as those used in its predecessor, the Skeeter, the major difference between the two types lying in the powerplant. Where the Skeeter was piston engined, the P 531 was powered by a Blackburn Turmo 603 shp turbine engine de-rated to 325 shp. In 1959, the Saunders-Roe company was taken over by Westland but development work on the P 531 continued. Westland constructed a further two prototype aircraft and up-rated the engines by replacing the Turmos with Blackburn Nimbus powerplants. Extensive flight trials were conducted with these helicopters in a series of deck landings both at the 'Rolling Platform' at the Royal Aircraft Establishment Bedford and aboard HMS *Undaunted* off the Dorset coast. After the conclusion of these trials it was obvious that the P 531 would become the Royal Navy's standard small ships' helicopter.

A major problem lay in the provision of a suitable undercarriage and to this end one or two novel ideas were evaluated. The first of these involved the fitting of four small suction pads to the landing skids. The idea called for negative air pressure to be applied to the pads via apparatus in the aircraft after landing, thus securing the helicopter to the deck. A positive air pressure was to be invoked for moving or air taxiing the machine. Sea trials with this ungainly apparatus were carried out aboard HMS *Undaunted* in 1961 although the system was later abandoned. The second idea was to replace the skids entirely with four long stroke legs fitted with fully castoring wheels and it was this system which, after successful testing, was adopted for production aircraft.

The first production Wasp flew on 28 October 1962 and the Royal Navy placed substantial orders for the type to operate from platforms on the aft end of 'Tribal', 'Rothesay' and 'Leander' class frigates. Wasps entered Fleet Air Arm service in late 1963, under control of 829 Squadron at Portland, Dorset. An exceptionally nimble helicopter, the Wasp operated as an extension of the parent ship's anti-submarine weapon system, although the machine itself carries no submersible detection equipment. For the attack role, standard armament is two Mk 44 homing torpedoes. This can be supplemented by 7.62-mm machine guns or Nord AS-12 wire-guided missiles if operating in a surface strike role. A neat and compact helicopter, the Wasp HAS Mk 1 has a main rotor diameter of 32 ft 3 in (9.83 m), a fuselage length of 30 ft 4 in (9.24 m) and a height of 11 ft 8 in (3.56 m). The Westland Wasp was also supplied to the navies of Brazil, Netherlands, South Africa, New Zealand and Indonesia.

In the Fleet Air Arm, the Wasp has provided outstanding service but although it has been used in roles from ice reconnaissance and search and rescue to liaison and anti-submarine strike, the type does not have the necessary endurance and payload for the increasingly complex naval operations of the 1980s. This problem has been resolved by the introduction of the Westland Lynx HAS 2 as the Wasp's replacement in Fleet Air Arm service.

The Lynx is a result of the joint Anglo-French helicopter agreement signed between Westland and Aérospatiale in 1967. Evolved from the Westland WG-13, the naval variant of the Lynx was first displayed to the world in 1966. Three initial naval prototypes were constructed, the first of these flying on 25 May 1972. By

An Aérospatiale SA 365F Dauphin 2 small ships' helicopter lifts off from the aft flight deck of a French warship.

this time, the helicopter had been formally named the Lynx and the Royal Navy ordered an initial batch of sixty aircraft. The type was also purchased by the French Aéronavale and the Royal Netherlands Navy and in September 1976, the Lynx Intensive Flying Trials Unit was formed at RNAS Yeovilton to carry out intensive pre-service testing of the Lynx in all its major roles. This unit was in fact unique in Royal Naval service since it was an Anglo-Dutch operation, the Royal Netherlands Navy having purchased the Lynx HAR 25, it was deemed more economic for the two countries to jointly operate one trials unit on a site close to the manufacturer's facility. The first Royal Naval Lynx became operational in December 1977, embarking in HMS *Sirius* as that ship's Flight.

Primary roles of this advanced helicopter are anti-submarine detection and strike, anti-surface ship strike, search and rescue, reconnaissance, stores supply, liaison and communications duties. Power is supplied by twin Rolls-Royce Gem 1,120 shp turboshaft engines, giving the semi-rigid rotor Lynx a performance of 200 mph maximum speed (322 km/h), a normal cruising speed of 144 mph (232 km/h) and a typical range with full payload of 336 miles (540 km). One advantage for a ship with a Lynx Flight is the harpoon deck lock grid system which consists of a retractable harpoon lock mounted in the belly of the helicopter which, after landing, engages in the deck mounted grid, thus providing positive locking of the aircraft to the flight deck in sea conditions of up to plus or minus 35 degrees of roll. As well as operating with the British and Dutch Navies, the Lynx is also in service with the naval air arms of Brazil, West Germany, Norway, France and Denmark.

Forerunner of the Wasp was the P531, seen here fitted with suction pad landing gear during sea trials.

Above *Standard Royal Navy small ship's helicopter before replacement with Lynx was the Westland Wasp. The aircraft in this photograph is fitted with weapon pylons for Nord AS 12 missiles and is seen lifting off the flight deck of a 'Rothesay' class frigate.*

Below *This Wasp serves with the South African Navy.*

Above *A Wasp helicopter of the Royal Netherlands Navy—the type has since been sold off to Indonesia.*

Below *This Wasp served with the Brazilian Navy before replacement with the Westland Lynx.*

Above *This Westland Scout was one of two examples purchased by the Royal Australian Navy for use aboard the hydrographic survey ship HMAS Moresby.*

Below *The Royal Navy Lynx can be fitted, as here, with four British Aerospace Dynamics 'Sea Skua' 'fire and forget' missiles. In May 1982 during the Falklands conflict a Fleet Air Arm Lynx equipped with these weapons attacked and disabled two Argentinian patrol vessels.*

Above *Westland's Navy Lynx is the world's only helicopter designed specifically for small ship operations. The Lynx is in service with nine maritime forces worldwide and the aircraft in this photograph is a Fleet Air Arm machine.*

Below *The cockpit of the Westland Lynx HAS 2.*

Above *This West German Navy Lynx is equipped with fail-safe wheel locks and harpoon deck lock, plus high energy absorbing undercarriage.*

Below *This Lynx of the Netherlands Navy prepares to dip its sonar.*

Above *The rotor head of the Lynx helicopter is forged from a single slab of titanium.*

Below *Close up of the Lynx observer's position. The main control visible is the 'Seaspray' radar display screen.*

Above *The naval variant of the Westland Lynx is now in squadron service with the Brazilian Navy: nine machines were ordered and commenced service in 1978.*

Below *A Norwegian Lynx.*

A Westland Lynx of the Argentinian Navy.

American counterparts

The standard small ships' helicopter in service with the US Navy is the Kaman H-2 Seasprite, the winner of a US Navy competition in 1956 for an all-weather ship based utility helicopter. The prototype aircraft flew for the first time on 2 July 1959, powered by a General Electric T58 1,025 shp turbine engine. The initial production of the Seasprite commenced with 88 of the UH-2A version in 1961. The first UH-2A Seasprites were delivered to the USN in December 1962 and the type first embarked for sea duty aboard USS *Independence* in June 1963. Operated by a two-man crew, the Seasprite flew on a range of duties that included casualty evacuation, search and rescue, 'plane guard', stores replinishment, reconnaissance and anti-submarine strike. Following the initial production batch of the A version, from August 1963 Kaman turned out a total of 102 UH-2B Seasprites, the major difference of this version over the A model being its electronics fit. In 1965, Kaman converted a UH-2B Seasprite to twin-engine configuration by fitting two General Electric turboshaft engines in pods either side of the main rotor mast. This resulted in a higher overall performance and payload and gave twin-engine reliability, a very reassuring factor for over-water operations. Commencing in 1967 the remainder of the preceding UH-2A and UH-2B aircraft were converted to twin-engine standard and were designated Seasprite UH-2C.

One of the US Navy's most important helicopter development programmes is the Light Airborne Multi Purpose System (LAMPS). LAMPS 1 equipped helicopters are used for anti-submarine and anti-ship missile direction and to this end Kaman modified many of the existing Seasprites to SH-2D standard. When the aircraft were converted to SH-2D standard new equipment fitted included a high power Marconi under-nose search radar, active and passive sonabuoys, homing torpedoes, flares, electronic counter measures equipment (ECM) and a magnetic anomaly detector (MAD). The first of these new conversions flew on 16 March 1971 and deployment to USN units began in the same year. The current version of the Seasprite is the SH-2F, which incorporates an improved radar system, a vibration-free main rotor and improved performance. The Seasprite helicopter is deployed aboard most modern USN ships. The Sikorsky SH-60B Seahawk was evolved from the US Army's UTTAS competition winner, the Sikorsky UH-60A Blackhawk and is the navalized version of that aircraft. The US Navy selected the type as its future ASW or LAMPS 3 air vehicle system helicopter in September 1977 and being basically similar to the Blackhawk, the SH-60B will become the US Navy's standard anti-submarine and anti-ship strike helicopter. Main changes to the naval aircraft are a re-designed cabin, the provision of automatic main rotor and tail rotor pylon folding for shipboard stowage, the fitting of MAD equipment, a high power surface search radar and 25 sonabuoy pneumatic launch tubes in the aircraft's port side.

The basically similar SH-60B Sea Hawk is the US Navy version of the Sikorsky Blackhawk.

The Aérospatiale SA 366 Dolphin is used by the US Coast Guard service for short range search and rescue and recovery missions.

Above *This neat helicopter is the Kaman Seasprite which for over twenty years has been the US Navy's standard ship-based anti-submarine warfare, rescue and utility aircraft.*

Below *The Sikorsky CH-53E is a heavy multi-purpose helicopter in service with the US Marine Corps and US Navy and is seen here lifting a damaged Lockheed S-3A Viking.*

Above *This twin-rotor Boeing Vertol CH-46 Sea Knight serves as a ship replenishment helicopter aboard the USS* Concord.

Below *The Sikorsky CH-53E operates in support of US Marine Corps amphibious operations.*

Soviet shipboard helicopters

The standard ship-borne helicopter of the Soviet Naval Air Force (AVMF) for many years has been the Kamov Ka-25. Known in the West by the NATO name Hormone, the Ka-25 was first seen by aviation observers at a Soviet aviation display near Moscow in July 1961. The primary role of the Ka-25 is that of anti-submarine warfare, although the type may also be employed on transport, liaison and search and rescue duties. A compact design, the helicopter follows the traditional Kamov layout with co-axial rotors atop one another, thus resulting in reduced rotor diameter for shipborne stowage and eliminating the need for an anti-torque tail rotor. Operated by a crew of three or four, the Hormone is powered by twin Glushenkov 900 shp turboshaft engines giving a maximum speed of 137 mph (220 km/h) and a range of around 400 miles (650 km). Major Soviet warships such as *Kiev* carry around 27 of the type, helicopter cruisers such as the *Leningrad* and *Moskva* eighteen each, the *Kirov* class five and cruisers such as the *Kara* or *Kresta* class, one or two. Around 200 Hormones are in service with the Soviet Navy, with others supplied to India for use aboard its *Krivak* cruisers and to Syria for coastal ASW patrols.

Recently observed in the West has been a new type of Kamov helicopter which has been allocated the NATO name Helix. Bearing a close resemblance to the Ka-25 Hormone, the Helix incorporates a larger cabin and probably increased operating performance. The type is expected to supplement the Ka-25 in Soviet naval service. Larger and more powerful than the Kamov helicopters is the Mil Mi 14 Haze which operates from shore bases in support of Soviet maritime operations and is believed to have been in service since 1977. Evolved from the Mil Mi 8 Hip troop transport helicopter, the Mi 14 is fitted with an amphibious flying boat-hull fuselage, stabilizing rear side floats and operates in the anti-submarine warfare role. Powered by twin Isotov 2,200 shp turbine engines the Mi 14 has more power available than its western counterpart, the Sea King.

Chapter 4

Search and Rescue

'Scramble Scramble ... Rambler trapped in mud by rising tide ... position one mile west of Reculver.' Out of the concrete pan that separates the aircraft hangars from the main runway, the duty helicopter pilot has already started the twin engines of the RAF Wessex and the drooping blades of the main rotor are starting to blur into a spinning disc. Having noted the above information and rescue co-ordinates the navigator and winchman sprint to the waiting aircraft, which within minutes of receiving the request for helicopter assistance, is airborne and on its way to the scene of the incident. To the general public it is for this work that the helicopter, particularly the military helicopter, is best known. Thanks to wide recognition through the medium of television and the national newspapers, search and rescue helicopters, their crews and their exploits appear regularly. Usually, however, only the briefest details of these missions are reported. What lies behind the few brief headlines in our morning newspaper or the short, dramatic statement on the evening newscast? Before describing some of the many actual rescues and mercy missions the helicopter has undertaken, let us first examine the background and organization of the search and rescue service.

The Royal Air Force regards the present military search and rescue (SAR) organization as having started in 1955 with the re-equipment of 22 and 202 Squadrons with helicopter types that were capable of performing SAR missions. The search and rescue organization of the RAF is controlled by No 18 Maritime Group, RAF Strike Command through two rescue co-ordination centres (RCCs). The southern RCC is located at Mount Wise near Plymouth and its northern equivalent at Pitreavie Castle, Dunfermline. Both of these centres are situated within a military complex, something of immediate benefit during a rescue incident when specialist equipment and communications may be required. The rescue co-ordination centre's primary responsibility is to provide a search and rescue service to handle military aviation incidents and thus the rescue of civilians, the type of work for which the search and rescue helicopter is best known, is purely secondary. In fact, the bulk of rescue work undertaken by the RCCs, some 80 per cent, comes from requests for assistance in civilian incidents. The Ministry of Defence has always reserved the right to charge for any of these services it provides. In practice however, the only charges normally made are those to an area health authority where an SAR helicopter is used to transfer a patient from one hospital to another. When dealing with rescues of the general public, the operation is normally classified as crew training and no charge is made.

In theory all requests for rescue helicopter assistance pass through the regional RCC, which co-ordinates all available resources to achieve the most effective use. Most of these requests come from Air Traffic Control Centres (ATCC) other RCCs or HM Coast Guard. Requests direct from the police force (who are bound by statutory regulations to respond to land incidents), the Royal National Lifeboat Institution (RNLI), Regional Health Authorities, shipping operators and mountain rescue teams are also accepted. The search and rescue helicopter units maintain a high state of readiness in preparation for response to military or civil incidents. A unit normally consists of four aircrew and 25 groundcrew. The usual SAR flight keeps one helicopter and its crew at fifteen minutes' readiness during daylight hours with a second machine and crew available at one hour's notice. Crews normally do 24 hours on fifteen minutes' or one hour's standby, fully dressed in flying kit and rubber immersion suits, with the helicopter pre-flighted and ready for immediate start up and lift-off. Search and rescue facilities of the RAF include two helicopter squadrons, 22 and 202, both with their headquarters at RAF Finningley near Doncaster, South Yorkshire.

Right *A Wessex Mk 2 rescue helicopter of 'E' Flight 22 Squadron RAF Manston, Kent lifts a 'stranded holidaymaker' from a cliff top during a training sortie.*

Below *The Sikorsky S-62 operates with the US Coast Guard service as the HH-52A. Some ninety aircraft are used by the service on search and rescue duties.*

Above *The Sikorsky S-61R or HH-3F operates with the US Coast Guard where the type is known as the Pelican on extended range search and rescue operations.*

Right *A civil Dragonfly winch—lifting a lifeboat man during a training sortie.*

Below *A Royal Air Force Wessex Mk 2 from the SAR flight of 22 Squadron Manston, Kent lifts a stretcher aboard during a simulated rescue exercise.*

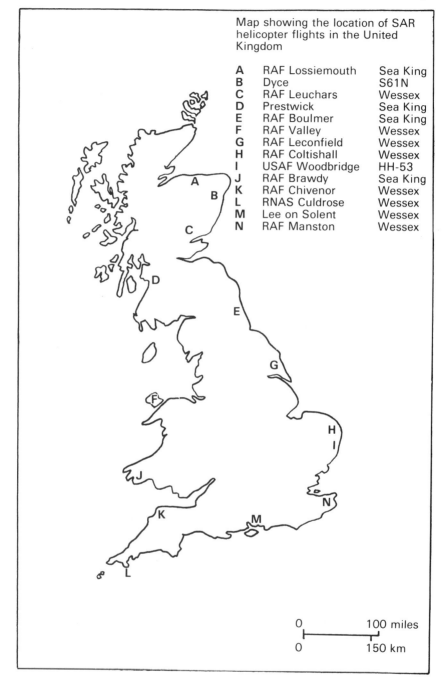

Map showing the location of SAR
helicopter flights in the United
Kingdom

A	RAF Lossiemouth	Sea King
B	Dyce	S61N
C	RAF Leuchars	Wessex
D	Prestwick	Sea King
E	RAF Boulmer	Sea King
F	RAF Valley	Wessex
G	RAF Leconfield	Wessex
H	RAF Coltishall	Wessex
I	USAF Woodbridge	HH-53
J	RAF Brawdy	Sea King
K	RAF Chivenor	Wessex
L	RNAS Culdrose	Wessex
M	Lee on Solent	Wessex
N	RAF Manston	Wessex

0 ————————— 100 miles

0 ————————— 150 km

Above *Photographed during a demonstration at Jarman's Boatyard near Sittingbourne, Kent, this winchman is signalling the winch operator/navigator in the RAF Wessex hovering above to stop the cable. He is seen 'walking on water' to stabilize himself prior to rescuing the 'survivor' with a double lift to the waiting helicopter.*
Left *Map showing the location of search and rescue helicopter flights in the United Kingdom.*

22 Squadron flies the twin-engined Westland Wessex HC Mk 2 with Flights stationed at the following airfields: Coltishall, Leuchars, Manston, Valley and Chivenor. Each of these Flights normally has two helicopters with a spare available at the squadron's headquarters. The other SAR squadron, No 202, operates the Westland Sea King HAR Mk 3 at three detached Flights at the following airfields: Brawdy, Boulmer and Lossiemouth. In addition, since the Falklands conflict, 202 Squadron has also maintained a detachment at RAF Stanley in the Falkland Islands. A flight crew is normally made up of three members, these being a pilot, navigator/winch operator and winchman in the Royal Air Force and pilot, observer/winch operator and winchman/diver in the Royal Navy.

Originally trained for planeguard duties when operating from aircraft carriers and commando carriers, the Navy has found the aircrewman/diver invaluable during over water rescue missions. He can be 'jumped' (the drop is normally made from around 20 ft with a forward airspeed of around 5-10 knots) directly from the helicopter to the stricken vessel, but the main advantage of the diver on these rescues is that he can carry out an underwater search for survivors and can be left behind in the water while the aircraft leaves the scene of the rescue with a full load. To cope with the variety and nature of possible incidents SAR crews spend a lot of their time training in both basic winching techniques and in more complex exercises with other rescue agencies.

The Neil Robertson stretcher and the NATO strop are the two main methods of effecting a rescue. The pilot and navigator, working in close co-operation, will position the helicopter directly over the casualty/person to be lifted. Because the pilot cannot see directly below the hovering helicopter, he relies on the navigator talking him into position. Once overhead the winchman/diver will be lowered to the casualty by the helicopter's 300 ft long winch cable. After administering any first aid that may be required (all rescue helicopters carry comprehensive first aid kits and oxygen equipment and more specialized 'kit' in the form of heart defibrillators can be loaded aboard and carried when needed) the winchman/ diver will recover the casualty to the aircraft using either the strop or stretcher. The Neil Robertson stretcher is a lightweight framework into which an injured person is strapped. To enable the helicopter crew to continue rescue operations under abnormal circumstances the winchman/diver and navigator are cross trained, each being able to act as winchman or winch operator. Downed military aircrew in need of rescue can also be picked up by means of a 'Grabbit' hook. This is a straightforward and simple hook with a 'Snap lock' mechanism which is attached to the winch cable. To effect a recovery using this method the hook is passed through lifting loops fitted on military lifejackets and the downed pilot is then winched aboard. This 'Grabbit' method of recovery is used only in conjunction with military lifejackets as there can be no way of knowing if a civilian lifejacket is capable of surviving the strain of a 'Grabbit' lift.

Search and Rescue Training Unit (SARTU)

'SARTU' is the helicopter search and rescue training unit of RAF Strike Command. As part of No 18 group's SAR wing the unit trains all RAF aircrew who man elements of search and rescue squadrons based around the shores of the United Kingdom. For pilot training the unit accepts pilots who have completed their basic training at No 2 Flying Training School at RAF Shawbury, who have completed their basic course of helicopter instruction and who have been awarded the flying brevet or 'wings'. The basic training for RAF helicopter pilots is 100 hours on fixed-wing training aircraft (Chipmunk/Bulldog and Jet Provost), 75 hours on Gazelles at RAF Shawbury then 50 hours on the Wessex, Puma or Chinook at the relevant operational conversion unit (OCU) at RAF Odiham, Hampshire. To be accepted for the course, potential RAF search and rescue pilots must be rated in their flying log books as of 'above average ability'. First tour pilots (those just out of flying training school) are not accepted for duty with SAR squadrons. Acceptance for SAR training can come only after a flying tour in a different role, say flying Pumas on tactical support duties. During the training period at the SARTU facility at RAF Valley, North Wales, the student pilot will undergo some twenty hours of role training and learn to rescue survivors from cliffs, the sea and from surface craft of the Royal Air Force Marine Craft Unit

Right *The Belgian Air Force operates five Mk 48 Sea King helicopters on SAR duties with No 40 Squadron.*

based at Holyhead. After successful completion of the course the student will be posted, either to a Wessex-equipped Flight or, following a course at the RAF Sea King Training Unit, as a co-pilot on a 202 Squadron Sea King.

The RAF Sea King Training Unit (RAFSKTU) is responsible for training pilots and rear crew members for flying duties with 202 Squadron, Royal Air Force. This squadron which is the RAF's specialist long range search and rescue squadron operates six Westland Sea King HAR 3s detached to three Flights around the UK. The RAFSKTU is based at the Royal Naval Air Station Culdrose in Cornwall and was formerly an integral part of 706 Naval Air Squadron (itself a Sea King training squadron tasked with the advanced training of student pilots who have been chosen for anti-submarine warfare duties) but manned mainly by RAF personnel. On 1 January 1982, however, the unit ceased to be part of 706 Squadron and became an independent RAF unit.

On operations the RAF Sea King has an operating crew of four, two pilots (one of whom is responsible for the aircraft's navigation), one radar operator, who also acts as the winch operator and one winchman who goes down on the wire to effect the rescue. The RAF Sea King Mk 3 differs from the Fleet Air Arm's Sea King helicopters by having larger fuel tanks giving the aircraft a greater operating

All RAF helicopter pilots, including those who will later fly search and rescue helicopters, complete their initial rotary wing training on the Westland/Aérospatiale Gazelle HT Mk3.

Above *Operating with 202 Squadron of the Royal Air Force is the Westland Sea King HAR Mk 3.*
Below *Westland Sea King Mk 43 helicopters of the Royal Norwegian Air Force. No 330 Squadron with headquarters at Bodo, operate ten of these aircraft on search and rescue duties along Norway's extensive coastline and into the North Sea.*

range, an improved avionics and navigational fit and a larger cabin which allows it to lift up to 22 survivors. On completion of the Sea King conversion course at Culdrose the SAR student is qualified as a Sea King captain. The rear crew training course lasts for ten weeks, during which time 58 hours are flown in the actual aircraft and over thirteen hours 'flown' in the Sea King simulator. From the service introduction of the Westland Sea King Mk 3 with 202 Squadron in 1978 up until the end of 1982 a total of 1,491 rescues had been made and in the course of those rescues, two George Medals, four Air Force Crosses, one British Empire Medal and three Queen's Commendations For Valuable Service in the Air have been awarded to RAFSKTU trained crews.

Rescue operations

None of the rotary-wing aircraft's many and varied applications catches the public's imagination quite as much as the lifesaver. The public has seen, for example, how sailors can be snatched to safety in conditions that are too difficult even for lifeboats, and they know, too, that the helicopter can usually get to the scene of an accident or natural disaster fastest, ready if necessary to fly out any injured straight to hospital or to fly in vital lifesaving supplies.

During the winter of 1962/63, Britain was hit by massive snow falls that blocked roads to such an extent that neither snowploughs nor any other type of clearing vehicle could cope with the task. For days on end heavy snow continued to fall, temperatures plunged lower by the hour and it was not surprising that local authorities, councils and police forces could not cope with the sheer intensity of the conditions. All over the country out-patients could not reach their local hospitals, food was running short in the shops and supermarkets but perhaps even more hard pressed than most were the farmers, whose sheep, pigs and other livestock were dying from starvation, exposure and frostbite. Clearing paths through the snow in attempts to get bales of feed through to these unfortunate animals was a thankless task. Not only a backbreaking chore, it also often proved fruitless, for as fast as a path was made, fresh falls of snow would fill in those areas already cleared. Only one thing could help the hard-pressed emergency services in these conditions—the helicopters of the Army Air Corps (mostly Alouettes of 6 Flight), the Royal Air Force and the Royal Navy.

One February morning during this period is typical. The duty crew of 'A' Flight of 22 Squadron at RAF Chivenor, Barnstaple, North Devon were watching the continually falling snow from the warmth of their crewroom. The weather forecast was the same as it had been for days—more falls of snow were expected, with winds gusting to gale force. Past experience had taught the SAR crews that their chances of being called out were greater the worse the weather became. It was not long before they were called into action. At 10.15 hours the telephone rang—a local farmer and a group of his farmhands had managed to dig their way through to a group of his trapped sheep but the animals were badly frostbitten and in dire need of veterinary treatment. The veterinary surgeon had managed to make it out to the farm, but could the Flight possibly help by providing a helicopter to lift the half dozen animals the mile or so back to the farm.

Above *Forerunner to the Wessex SAR helicopter was the Westland Whirlwind Mk 10 seen here during a continuation training sortie.*

Below *Search and rescue Whirlwind helicopters of the Royal Air Force.*

After obtaining the position of the stranded flock and giving an assurance that they would do their best, the Whirlwind lifted off in a flurry of snow. It was after lift-off that the crew's difficulties began. The driving snow had brought the cloudbase down to almost ground level and in these conditions the only method of navigating was by the 'IFR' method. The initials 'IFR' normally refer to Instrument Flight Rules, but in these conditions they were substituted for 'I Follow Roads'. Thus, with the bright yellow Whirlwind skimming the trees above remote country lanes, the crew gingerly felt their way across the snow-ravaged countryside. The villages of Punchardon and Pippacott came and went in the white mist, until after a while the farm at Guineaford loomed into view. The snowstorm had increased in intensity and the swirling whiteness obliterated all view beyond 50 yards or so. After landing beside the farmhouse to pick up the vet and ask directions to the farmer's position, the helicopter finally arrived at the animals' location, almost thirty minutes after the initial departure from base. After negotiating a barbed wire fence the somewhat disconcerted sheep were manhandled by the vet and the winchman into the Whirlwind's main cabin. When all six sheep, the vet, the farmer and his three hands and finally the winchman were secured aboard, the helicopter lifted off for the short flight back to the farm. By this time it was starting to snow heavily again and the windows in the cockpit were quickly icing up. To counter this the pilot slid open his side window,

A piston-engined Westland Whirlwind Mk 2 hovers for the camera.

kicked in a bootful of left anti-torque pedal and 'crabbed' the helicopter slowly through the blinding murk back to safety. With the animals now safe and after a warming drink at the farmhouse, it was once again an 'IFR' flight back to base at Chivenor.

Most rescues are performed by specialist crews but all helicopter aircrew are trained in search and rescue techniques and any Royal Air Force, Royal Navy, Army Air Corps or civilian helicopter can be used to help save life and property in an emergency, as occurred for example in the operation that began on 25 December 1973.

On the morning of Christmas Day 1973, the 159,000 ton freighter the *Elwood Mead* with 123,000 tons of iron ore aboard ran on to reefs two miles north-west of Guernsey. It was initially feared that she would be a total loss, but after a number of salvage firms had examined the wreck, Wijsmuller's of Ijmuiden, Holland decided that the job could be undertaken and engaged the Bristow Helicopter Group to help them. In the conditions prevailing around the stricken ship no other vessel could be relied on to get alongside. In the nine weeks that followed, Westland Wessex helicopters of the Bristow company flew more than 500 salvage personnel to and from the ship and more than 230,000 lb of salvage equipment, over 95 per cent of this being underslung. The helicopters not only ferried the vital compressors and pumps out to the ship, but lifted them from hold to hold on a 120 ft long strop. Eventually with 30,000 tons of her cargo removed and compressed air being forced into her at the rate of 3,000 cubic feet a minute, the *Elwood Mead* was refloated and towed up the English Channel to Rotterdam, where a dry dock was waiting for her.

Whilst engaged in the *Elwood Mead* operation one of the Bristow aircraft was called upon to offer timely assistance in a second wreck drama. The timber ship *Prosperity* had been driven on to a nearby reef and many crew members were missing. Five St John Ambulance men succeeded in getting aboard the ship to search for the missing men, but their motor dinghy was also tossed on to the nearby reef by a wave. An emergency flare brought the Bristow helicopter to their rescue within minutes.

Army helicopters are not allocated a specific rescue function, but on the night of 6 June 1977 a Westland Scout AH 1 aircraft on a routine anti-terrorist patrol was requested to assist in the search for a small cruiser missing on Lough Erne in County Fermanagh, Northern Ireland. The missing cruiser was duly spotted by the Scout, lying aground on rocks with waves and 30 knot winds breaking over it. The Army aircraft positioned itself in a precise hover with its skid undercarriage touching the boat's cabin roof and the four cold and wet survivors were assisted aboard the Scout by the aircrewman.

On 1 February 1978 two Sea King helicopters from RNAS Culdrose were scrambled at 23.00 hours to Guernsey where the oil rig *Orion*, on tow to Brazil, had run aground. Despite the mountainous seas, very high winds and the dangerous oscillation of the rig, 25 men were rescued that night before further attempts were abandoned. Two men were rescued by breeches-buoy the following morning and the remaining four men were lifted off by the Sea Kings.

In almost eleven hours of flying time, the two Sea King helicopters had rescued 29 men and the pilots, Lieutenants Robert Davidson, Tony Eagles, Glen Tilsley and Paul Crudgington later received Air Force Crosses for their parts in the *Orion* rescue.

Fleet Air Arm Sea King helicopters from the Culdrose Naval Air Station played a vital part in the salvage attempt mounted when the Greek oil tanker *Christos Bitas* ran aground on rocks off the South Wales coast. During the eighteen days of the operation, which began on 13 October 1978, helicopters from Culdrose flew a total of 92 hours on 42 separate sorties.

On 31 December 1978, at night in a force ten gale, with visibility reduced to 50 yards by blinding snow blizzards, aircrew of 814 Naval Air Squadron in their Westland Sea Kings were 'talked' into a cove backwards by coastguards positioned on the clifftop, to snatch eight crew members of the trawler *Ben Asdale*

Shell Expro's air sea and rescue service in the Brent area of the North Sea 110 miles north-east of Shetland, was created during the summer of 1979 in close co-operation with Bristow Helicopters and Solus Ocean. Personnel from both organizations underwent training as winch crewman followed by a conversion course on Bell helicopters. The rescue service which includes fast inflatable surface craft is provided primarily for Expro's own operations but it will respond to any distress call within reach. Weekend practice sessions are held in the Brent area when operational flying activities are at their lowest level. It was on one of these occasions that this photograph was taken in October 1979. The rescue helicopter is a Bristow Bell 212 and it is seen preparing to land on the rig Tresure Finder.

from certain death. For this rescue three of the aircrew received gallantry awards.

The Fastnet rescue operations of 14, 15 and 16 August 1979 heavily involved the Culdrose Naval Air Station and the Wessex 5 helicopters of 771 Squadron. Yachtsmen were caught in sudden storm force weather conditions during the 1979 Fastnet race. This was the Culdrose station's largest rescue operation and helicopters were airborne for a total of 203 hours during the three days and rescued 73 survivors from the 30-40 ft wave conditions.

17 May 1980 saw an unusual operation for aircrew of 771 Squadron. A herd of cows stampeded over a cliff near Portholland and were in imminent danger of being drowned by the incoming tide. In a desperate race against time, twelve of the stricken animals were lifted to safety on the cliff top by a 771 Squadron Wessex 5.

The cargo ship the *Finneagle* on the night of 2 October 1980 was 50 miles north-west of the Orkney Islands when a sudden explosion set the vessel on fire amidships. On receipt of distress calls from the stricken ship a British Airways Helicopters' Sikorsky S-61N and the duty search and rescue Sea King at RAF Lossiemouth were scrambled. A second Sea King piloted by Flight Lieutenant

The Westland Whirlwind HAR Mk 9 was the Royal Navy's equivalent of the RAF Mk 10. The HAR Mk 9 was mainly based at RNAS Lee on Solent, Culdrose and Brawdy on search and rescue operations, although the type also served at sea aboard HMS Protector *and HMS* Endurance *on ice patrol duties in the Antarctic.*

Michael Lakey also arrived at the scene and was informed that the BAH S-61N had attempted to rescue the ship's crew, although the aircraft was not fitted with suitable rescue equipment for the terrible weather conditions. The first RAF Sea King had attempted to winch aboard the crew members, but had also been unsuccessful and had to divert to Kirkwell Airfield to refuel. The weather that night was appalling. Waves were topping 70 feet and the winds were gusting to over 70 knots. At around 02.00 hours Lakey's Sea King attempted a rescue. The scene of the rescue was only illuminated by the Sea King's own spotlights (the *Finneagle* having lost all electrical power) and the glow from the fire and intermittent explosions of the vessel itself.

Establishing a hover perilously close to the pitching superstructure of the ship, an attempt was made to lower the winchman, Sergeant Richard Bragg, to the heaving deck. Because of the danger and difficulty of holding the helicopter in a precise hover so close to the pitching masts, the attempt was unsuccessful. A second attempt was then made to lift off survivors, this time using the 'High Line' method. (See diagram.) Eventually this proved successful and just as the first survivors came aboard the Sea King, the ship rose upwards on a huge wave so close to the hovering helicopter that the pilot was forced to take rapid avoiding action. The remaining members of the ship's crew were eventually lifted aboard during a total of almost two hours winching. Finally with 27 people including the crew aboard the Sea King, the helicopter headed back to the safety of the shore. For this rescue the crew were all awarded gallantry decorations. The Sea King captain, Flight Lieutenant Michael Lakey, was awarded the George Medal, Flight Lieutenant David Simpson, the co-pilot, the Queen's Commendation For Valuable Service in the Air, Flight Lieutenant Thomas Campbell, the winch and radar operator, the Air Force Cross, Sergeant Richard Bragg the winchman, the Air Force Medal and the senior doctor of RAF Lossiemouth who was aboard that night, Squadron Leader Hamish Grant, received the Queen's Commendation For Brave Conduct.

A typical case of inter-rescue service co-operation occurred on 14 November 1980 when the fishing vessel *Pietje Antje* foundered in heavy seas off Start Point. Three survivors were rescued from a liferaft by a passing merchant ship. Two Westland Sea Kings from 706 Naval Air Squadron searched for over seven hours and located two further men in another liferaft. Since the sea conditions at the time were too high for them to be safely recovered aboard the helicopters, the Sea Kings 'homed' the Torbay lifeboat to the scene to effect the rescue operation.

On 19 September 1981 a Sea King helicopter of 706 Naval Air Squadron and the Sennen lifeboat combined forces to rescue the eleven-man crew of the Icelandic vessel *Tungufoss* which was foundering in the mountainous seas off Lands End. The helicopter rescued three of the crew members, then used its powerful floodlights to illuminate the scene while the lifeboat moved in to rescue a further seven men from liferafts and the sinking vessel itself. The Sea King then snatched the last man to safety literally as the ship began to turn over and sink beneath him. The coxswain of the lifeboat was later awarded the RNLI's Silver Medal.

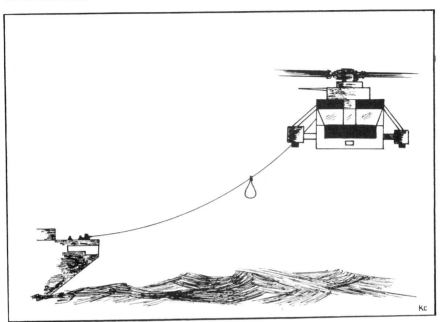

The Hi-Line transfer system.

13 December 1981 saw a Sea King helicopter of 814 Squadron and a Wessex 5 of 771 Squadron scrambled to lift off the ship's crew of the Ecuadorean freighter *Bonita* which was sinking in heavy seas and 60 mph winds in the English Channel. Although the 771 Squadron Wessex had to force land at Dartmouth, having been damaged in the snowstorm, the Sea King managed to reach the scene and provide illumination with its powerful floodlights while the lifeboat from St Peter Port, Guernsey, snatched 29 crew members to safety. Another helicopter and a French tug later rescued six others. The Sea King, having been airborne for over six hours, was then diverted to go to the assistance of the coaster *Bobrix* and its six-man crew. This ship had developed a list and was sinking forty miles to the west. Despite the darkness and the violent pitching of the ship in the rough seas, this rescue was successfully accomplished and the helicopter touched down back at the Royal Naval Air Station Culdrose nine hours after first being scrambled.

Six days later, in gusting winds of up to 100 mph, the eight-man crew of the Penlee lifeboat the *Soloman Browne* and a Fleet Air Arm Sea King helicopter crew battled to try to save the eight people aboard the stricken freighter the *Union Star*. The vessel, with a cargo of fertilizer bound for Dublin on her maiden voyage, had broken down with engine failure eight miles off Lands End. As she drifted for over two hours, waves reached 70 ft and the powerful winds gusted to over 85 knots. Eventually she was washed ashore onto rocks and overturned. Repeated attempts were made by the helicopter crew to winch the survivors aboard—unfortunately these were unsuccessful. In the subsequent tragic disaster the lifeboat, having reported recovering four persons from the ship, went in again in an attempt to pick up more. Thrown against the side of the overturned ship, all sixteen lives aboard the lifeboat were lost.

On 2 April 1983, in the largest sea rescue off Mount's Bay since the destruction of the Penlee lifeboat and the freighter *Union Star*, all the emergency services were called into action in the early hours of the morning to go to the aid of the 4,700 ton Brittany Ferries Liner *Armorique* with over 700 passengers aboard. In the accommodation section a fire had broken out and one man, a school teacher from Brittany, had died in the blaze. A further eleven passengers were winched to safety and flown to hospital in Penzance suffering from the effects of toxic fumes and burns. The drama had begun ten miles north of the Seven Stones lightship between Lands End and the Isles of Scilly and by 06.30 hours a massive co-ordinated rescue was underway. A Wessex 5 helicopter from 771 Naval Air Squadron was scrambled with a fire-fighting team, breathing apparatus and foam extinguishers to help tackle the blaze. On arrival the Naval firemen were winched down and two casualties, a girl of six and her father were lifted aboard in Neil Robertson stretchers and flown to hospital. Throughout the rest of the day the Senen and new Penlee lifeboats took over the task of ferrying people, fire-fighting equipment and medical supplies to and fro between the ship and Penzance. Eventually eighty passengers and crew had to be lifted off the ship and brought ashore before the fire was under control.

The duty Wessex 5 helicopter of 771 Squadron was airborne on 28 September 1983 on a routine training mission when it was diverted to check on a 27 ft sloop by the name of *Telic*. There were two crew members aboard and, although not in immediate danger, they had sustained a certain amount of damage in the rough weather. The vessel was sighted and contact by radio was made. The husband and wife aboard had had little sleep since the 22nd and were not capable of bringing the yacht into Falmouth. It was requested that a yachtsman be flown out to take over the vessel. The Wessex returned to Culdrose, refuelled and collected two auxiliary coastguards who had volunteered to go out and bring the yacht into harbour. When the search and rescue Wessex arrived back at the yacht the weather had worsened to gale conditions with 20 foot waves. The helicopter's aircrewman/diver was 'jumped' from the aircraft ahead of the yacht and climbed aboard to brief the crew about the transfer of the coastguards. After some difficult winching, the coastguards were transferred and crew and diver recovered aboard the helicopter, which then returned to Culdrose. The *Telic* sailed safely into Falmouth harbour that evening.

On 27 October 1983 whilst airborne on a training sortie, the duty search and rescue Wessex from Culdrose received a VHF radio message from the Maritime Rescue Co-ordination Centre (MRCC), requesting helicopter assistance for a person reported to have been swept off the pier by heavy seas at Mullian. When the helicopter arrived at the scene, a man was quickly sighted 20 yards off the pier, lying face down in the water. While the aircraft maintained a steady hover, the aircrewman/diver was winched down to get a NATO strop around the unconscious man. He was then double lifted aboard the helicopter and flown to

Treliske hospital. En route the casualty was treated by a medical assistant and showed signs of improvement. After a short stay in hospital the man made a full recovery.

Not all of the rescue missions undertaken by helicopters fall into the accepted search and rescue role. One outstanding flight amongst these non-designated flights was operation 'Frequent Wind', the largest helicopter civil rescue mission in history. When the Americans ordered the evacuation of Saigon, operation 'Frequent Wind' was the code name given to the plan to lift out all United States citizens, dependants, 'third country nationals' and those Vietnamese people having a 'special relationship' with the USA. This plan was said to have been the largest helicopter evacuation ever and among the aircraft that took part were ten Boeing Vertol CH-46 Sea Knights, 35 Sikorsky CH-53 heavy lift helicopters, eight Bell Cobras and numerous Bell Hueys. All these helicopters were based on ships of the United States Navy's Seventh Fleet, which had been lying off the Vietnamese coast, waiting for the order to go, for nine days. Evacuees were to be set down on US carriers and other major surface vessels and would then be distributed among the fifty or so other ships within the fleet.

The evacuation commenced at 14:30 on 29 April 1975 and the first civilians were flown out to the waiting ships at 15:00 on the same afternoon. One of the major pick up points for the helicopters was the US Embassy compound in Saigon. Here US Marine Corps CH-53 aircraft landed in the car park, while the lighter twin rotor Sea Knights used the roof-top helipad. The Marine helicopter pilots reported small arms fire upon landing in the Embassy compound and indeed a number of aircraft, particularly CH-53s, were damaged as

Boeing Vertol CH-46 Sea Knight helicopters helped rescue 7,400 evacuees from Saigon during operation 'Frequent Wind' the biggest helicopter rescue mission in history.

a result. One of the most well remembered moments of the operation which was extensively covered by news film crews at the time was the arrival of various types of South Vietnamese Air Force and Army helicopters aboard the US ships. Immediately upon landing the Vietnamese helicopters were pushed overboard because the flight deck space was urgently needed to receive yet more incoming aircraft. In all over fifty helicopters, mainly Hueys, were ditched. By the time the great evacuation ceased around 08.00 hours on 30 April 1975, over 590 sorties had been flown and over 7,400 evacuees had been airlifted out to the waiting ships.

Chapter 5

Civil helicopters

Until quite recently the helicopter has been regarded primarily as a military flying machine. The world's armed forces have been using helicopters for several decades to transport troops, to hunt submarines, to attack tanks and armoured vehicles and to fly search and rescue missions. In all of these operations the expensive operating costs have been borne out of huge military budgets. Traditionally, what civil helicopters have been available, have been spin-offs from successful military types. Civil helicopters have taken a long time to appear in any number principally because the aircraft has to make a profit for the civil operator. This was not easy, for initially most civilian machines were derived from military models. Of course to attempt to use the helicopter in competition with the fixed-wing aeroplane on most passenger routes is clearly economically ridiculous. This basic fact however did not deter a number of national airlines during the 1950s from playing with helicopters on subsidized internal domestic passenger routes.

One of the earliest scheduled helicopter services was started by the then British European Airways on 1 June 1950, using three Westland Dragonfly aircraft. It operated between Liverpool and Cardiff with an optional stop at Wrexham and during the ten months of its operation the three aircraft carried a total of 819 passengers over the route. One of the major obstacles to further development of inter-city routes or civil operations at all has been the attitude of the general public to the helicopter. In the United Kingdom the helicopter is still something of a novelty, something only seen on television or read about in the morning newspapers in a dramatic search and rescue operation. When a helicopter does appear at close hand, particularly above a city centre, it draws attention and any noise it makes is largely exaggerated.

This public attitude towards helicopter noise is mostly psychological—noise is just something they associate with helicopters. In tests, rotary-wing aircraft noise has proved indiscernible among the trains, traffic and general bustle of a busy city. The City of London enjoyed a brief inter-city scheduled helicopter service during the mid-1950s when BEA helicopters operated a Westland Whirlwind between a landing site on the south bank of the Thames and Heathrow Airport. During the period of operation, July 1955 to May 1956, over 3,800 fare-paying passengers bought seats on this route, in spite of petty regulations which required the helicopter to be fitted with pontoon floats in case of an emergency landing on its River Thames route, a massive exhaust silencer running down one complete side of the aircraft to cut down noise and, of all things, an anchor. Final attempts by BEA during the 1950s again involved the use of a Whirlwind, this time operating between Leicester, Nottingham and Birmingham (Elmdon) Airport. Unfortunately passenger traffic was extremely low and the service was terminated after only five months of operations in November 1956.

Across the North Atlantic, American helicopter airlines were enjoying a much more successful existence. Thanks to the greater distances and the number of small commuter airline services, the American public is much more used to air travel. The City of New York has operated a number of inter-city helicopter services, one of the earliest and more successful being New York Airways. On 1 July 1962 New York Airways brought the first of its twin-rotor passenger carrying Boeing Vertol 107 helicopters into operation on a flying-taxi service between John F. Kennedy International Airport and the Wall Street heliport in downtown Manhattan. The prototype Boeing Vertol 107 helicopter had made its maiden flight on 22 April 1958 and was designed to accommodate 25 passengers and a flight crew of three (two pilots and a stewardess). Power was supplied by a pair of

The Westland Widgeon was a further development of the Dragonfly. The cockpit was redesigned to hold a pilot and four passengers and some fifteen aircraft were produced for civil customers and various export orders.

Above *The inauguration of the Pest Control Helicopter Spraying Service with a Dragonfly at Bourn Aerodrome in June 1948.*

Below *An Aérospatiale SA 315 Lama hovers to pick up an underslung load of fertilizer during agricultural operations in Scotland.*

Above *This Fairchild FH-1100 is a five-seat civil utility helicopter developed from the Hiller OH-5A military observation aircraft.*

Below *A VIP passenger for this British Caledonian Sikorsky S-61N in the summer of 1982 during his British tour was Pope John Paul II.*

Above *A civil Westland Whirlwind equipped with floatation gear.*

Below *The British European Airways 'BEA' helicopter unit operated the Westland Whirlwind on scheduled services between Leicester, Nottingham and Birmingham's Elmdon Airport in 1956. Unfortunately passenger traffic was very poor and the service was abandoned after only five months of operations.*

General Electric 1,250 shp CT-58-110-1 turboshaft engines driving tandem main rotors of 50 ft (15.24 m) diameter. A large aircraft, the fuselage length was 44 ft 7 in (13.59 m), height was 16 ft 8½ in (5.09 m) and maximum speed at a service ceiling of 13,000 ft (3,960 m) was 157 mph (253 km/h). This service almost immediately began to show an operating profit, largely due to the fact that by taxi the journey between the two destinations took one hour and cost $5.00. The helicopter, at a cost of $8.00, covered the same distance in just seven minutes.

In the United Kingdom today, there is a successfully operated scheduled passenger and freight helicopter service, run by British Airways Helicopters, between Penzance, near Land's End and the Isles of Scilly. Outside of the United States the largest operator of helicopters on passenger-carrying routes is the Soviet state airline, Aeroflot. In Russia, particularly in Siberia, large numbers of helicopters, including the giant Mil Mi 6, Mi 8 and Mi 17 operate services with

The Rotodyne was a helicopter in advance of its time, but was doomed as soon as British politicians took an interest in it. A combination of conventional helicopter and fixed-wing airliner it would have been an admirable heavy lift helicopter or inter-city transport. Powered by rotor tip pressure jets it set a number of speed records over a closed circuit course in 1959. Despite interest from the Royal Air Force and British European Airways as potential customers, the British government, as with so many other outstanding aircraft of the period, got cold feet, and after spending millions of pounds of taxpayers' money, abandoned the aircraft.

fares, which are generally paid out of state taxes thus removing the need for profitable operation, around the same cost as rail or fixed-wing aeroplane travel.

Business helicopters

Only since the turboshaft engine was first fitted to small helicopters in the mid-1950s have we seen the development of helicopters as useful tools of transport for the business company executive or private individual. The same company that installed that first Artouste turboshaft into the Alouette 2 light helicopter is today the largest manufacturer of civil helicopters in Europe. One in four helicopters in the world is built by that company, Aérospatiale, and over 7,500 aircraft have been sold to nearly 600 operators in over 100 countries. Aérospatiale has built a dozen different types of civil turbine powered helicopters ranging from the tiny SO-1221 Djinn up to the three engined SA-321 Super Frelon. The most important small business helicopters now marketed by Aérospatiale are the AS-350 Ecureuil and the SA-365 Dauphin 2.

Intended as a replacement aircraft for the highly successful but now somewhat dated Alouette series, the AS-350 Ecureuil (or Squirrel) is the European equivalent of the Bell 206 JetRanger. This delightful six-seat general purpose helicopter first took to the air on 27 June 1974, powered by a single 641 shp Turbomeca Arriel turboshaft engine. It has a fuselage length of 35 ft 9½ in (10.91 m) rotors turning, a rotor diameter of 35 ft ¾ in (10.69 m), a maximum speed of 169 mph (272 km/h) and an operating range of 460 miles (740 km). Of particular interest on the Squirrel is the rotor head system. Known as the 'Starflex hub', this is largely made of plastic and the conventional rotor blade hinges are replaced with a single steel/rubber ball joint that requires no maintenance. The whole assembly consists of only 64 parts compared with the Gazelle (another Aérospatiale product) which has over 200. The type is in wide use as a company air-taxi aircraft, general charter helicopter and as a police and medivac machine with the French Gendarmerie.

The SA-365N Dauphin 2 is a much larger helicopter, with twin turbine engines and seating for up to fourteen passengers. First flown on 24 January 1975, the Dauphin 2 is a twin-engined version of the earlier SA-360 Dauphin. Two Turbomeca Arriel 1C 650 shp free-turbine turboshafts drive a four-bladed main rotor of 38 ft 4 in (11.68 m) diameter giving the aircraft a maximum speed of 196 mph (315 km/h) and an operating range of 345 miles (555 km). The Dauphin 2 not only incorporates a Starflex rotor head, but also has the Fenestron ducted fan anti-torque rotor familiar from the Gazelle light helicopter. The Dauphin 2 is a popular company transport with large organizations such as the Trafalgar House Group and Sony Corporation but it is also used for oilfield support duties with Bond Helicopters (formally North Scottish Helicopters) on the North Sea.

Perhaps the most successful of all small civil helicopters and certainly one of the prettiest is the Bell Model 206. This began life as a military prototype, the OH–4A, as an entrant in the US Army's Light Observation Helicopter (LOH) contest of 1962, in competition with the Hughes Helicopter OH–6A. When Bell lost the contract to Hughes, the OH–4A was launched afresh into the civil market as the

JetRanger. Bell swiftly made bold predictions for their new machine, forecasting that it would capture a bigger market share than any other helicopter, civil or military, before it. The company was soon proved correct when the JetRanger started selling like hot cakes. Ironically, Bell later won a huge military order with the JetRanger, when in 1968 the US Army re-opened the Light Observation Helicopter contest and awarded Bell the contract to build 2,200 OH-58A Kiowas. As a follow on to this huge order, the Model 206 was also supplied to the US Navy, the Canadian Armed Forces and the military air arms of Australia, Sweden, Jamaica, Turkey and Spain to name but a few.

It was largely with an eye to the civil market however that the JetRanger was constantly improved and refined; the Model 206A was superseded in production from 1971 by the Model 206B JetRanger 2. This was itself superseded in 1977 by the introduction of the JetRanger 3, powered by an uprated Allison 250-C20B 420 shp turbine and including a number of improvements particularly to the main and tail rotor systems. It was for the civil JetRanger that Bell developed its patented 'Noda-Matic' suspension to minimize the vibration that has always been an inherent problem with helicopters. This system allows the helicopter to be suspended from its rotor hub by a 'nodalised beam' which effectively dampens out vibration from the rotor system before it can reach the airframe. Today, as much as when it first appeared, the JetRanger is the most popular helicopter among air-taxi and charter operators.

This Columbia Hiller helicopter has been converted to turbine power by the installation of an Allison turboshaft engine.

Above *The Westland 606 was a civil version of the Lynx with a spacious main cabin for up to twelve passengers, with an extra passenger in the front left hand seat of the cockpit. This good-looking helicopter did not, unfortunately, go into production.*

Below *The Robinson R 22 is increasingly popular with civilian flight schools for basic helicopter flying training.*

Above *The Sud-Aviation Djinn was the world's first production helicopter to be powered by 'cold jet' propulsion. This is where compressed air from the turbine engine is pumped through pipes inside the rotor blades and expelled through nozzles at the blade tips. Main customer for this remarkable little machine was the French Army whose aviation units took delivery of 150 of the type.*

Left *The cockpit of the Robinson R 22 light training helicopter.*

Below *Cut-away drawing of the MBB BK 117 lightweight, twin-engined 8–11 seat multipurpose helicopter.*

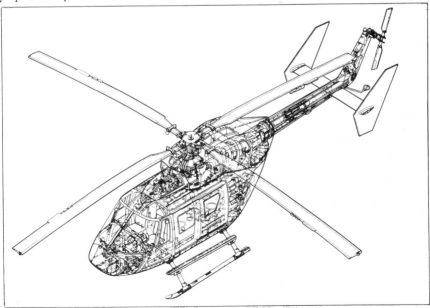

Above *Like the Gazelle, this SA 365N Dauphin 2 light civil helicopter is fitted with a Fenestron tail rotor.*

Below *This Aerospatiale Alouette 3 was operated by Iranian Helicopters.*

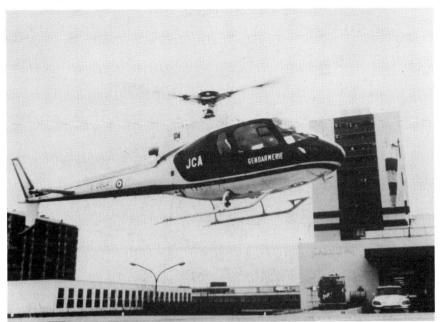

Above *This AS 350B Ecureuil operates with the French Gendarmerie—the Para Military.*

Below *This attractive Hughes 500C, G-HSKY, is operated by Skyline Helicopters Ltd and is available at Booker Airfield for self-fly charter by qualified helicopter pilots.*

Above *Basically an enlarged version of the two-seat model B2, the Brantly 305 is a five-seat light civil helicopter powered by a 305 hp Lycoming piston engine and the type can be fitted with a wheel, twin-float or skid undercarriage. The aircraft in this photograph is an Icelandic registered machine.*

Below *The Spitfire Taurus is an American-designed helicopter based on the Soviet Mil Mi 2.*

Above *Developed from the Lynx the Westland 30 is a civil and military transport helicopter seen here in Westland demonstration markings.*

Below *An early Westland/Aérospatiale Gazelle lifts off on a demonstration flight. In the background one can see Alouette 3, Puma, Lama and Super Frelon helicopters.*

Above *The Spitfire Mk 2 is a turbine-powered helicopter based on the piston-engined Enstrom F-28A and is still under development.*

Left *The cockpit layout of a civil Gazelle helicopter, clearly visible are the cyclic control stick and anti-torque pedals.*

Below *An impression of the Spitfire Mk 4 compound helicopter.*

Above *The delightful lines of the Bell 206 JetRanger are clearly shown in this unusual photograph.*

Right *At work in the vast Canadian forests this JetRanger is burning waste wood known as slush, after logging operations.*

Below *This JetRanger 3 is from Alan Mann Helicopters of Fairoaks in Surrey, part of the Alan Mann Group of Companies who operate one of the largest fleets of business charter JetRanger helicopters in the United Kingdom. The turbine-powered JetRanger cruises at around 125 mph and from Fairoaks Airport, London's Heathrow is approximately five minutes flying time, Gatwick fifteen minutes and Battersea Heliport in central London, ten minutes.*

Above *The Bell 206 LongRanger is a seven-seat helicopter developed from the five-seat model 206B JetRanger 2. Clearly visible on the landing skids are the 'pop out' floats which allow the helicopter to land on water in an emergency.*

Below *A fine study of an Agusta 109 helicopter with St Paul's Cathedral in the background.*

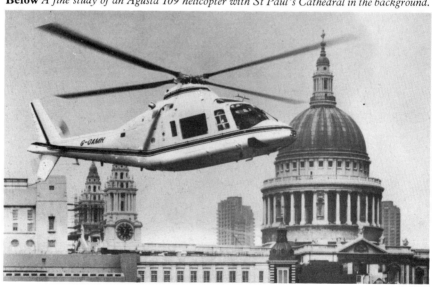

Above *The Rotorway Exec is a light two-seat American helicopter designed to be built at home from a kit by amateur aircraft constructors.*

Below *This photograph of a light two-place Brantly B2 helicopter shows off the type's unique rotor design which incorporates an extra flapping hinge and lag hinge at approximately 40 per cent of blade span, something found on no other make of helicopter.*

Policing from the air

Major users of civil helicopters are the police forces of various nations. In the United Kingdom, the Metropolitan Police have for many years been aware of the value of eyes in the sky in certain situations. As far back as 1921, the police borrowed the Airship *R33* from the Air Ministry to keep an aerial watch on crowds and traffic at that year's Derby race meeting. Over the years that followed there were experiments with autogyros, balloons and fixed-wing aircraft, but it was not until 1967 that a number of police forces began to seriously examine the possibilities of using helicopters in their work. Over the next ten years, the Metropolitan Police made more and more use of hired helicopters, mainly three-seat light piston-engined Enstrom F-28s, until it became worthwhile to look at the possibility of purchasing their own machine.

During the 1970s, the Metropolitan Police had been granted special permission by the Civil Aviation Authority (CAA) to operate single-engined machines over Central London, an agreement that came to an end in 1980. This meant that the first aircraft the force bought would have to be a twin-engined helicopter, and so a Bell 222 was purchased (after a long evaluation of types which included the Aérospatiale SA 365C, Agusta 109, MBB 105 and Sikorsky S-76) and a second aircraft went into service in June 1981. Powered by two Avco Lycoming LTS-101-650-C2 675 shp turboshaft engines, the prototype 222 first flew on 13 August 1976. In addition to a maximum speed of 165 mph (265 km/h) and an operating range with twenty minute reserves of 325 miles (523 km) other features of this streamlined helicopter include under-nose glazing for downward view during rooftop landings, stub wings to carry the retractable undercarriage and Bell's 'Noda-Matic' suspension for a smoother ride.

The two Metropolitan Police helicopters are part of the Air Support Unit, based at Lippitts Hill in open country near Epping Forest, Essex and facilities here include a hangar, a control room overlooking the landing pad, service bays, workshops and stores. From this base either helicopter can be anywhere over the Metropolitan Police area within fifteen minutes' flying time. The basic flying pattern for the unit's helicopters is three routine patrols of about $1\frac{1}{2}$ hours each weekday for each machine. During the weekends and evenings the helicopters are available on an 'as required' basis. In an emergency, either of the Bell 222s can be in the air at very short notice at any time of the day or night. The list of police operations in which the aircraft may be called upon for help is endless: crowd control, traffic control, searching and pursuing and any situations in which observation from the air is of special value are all part of the helicopters' daily workload. A normal day's flying operations recently included going to the scene of an armed robbery in South London, observing the build up of a traffic jam on a North London main road and a search for a stolen heavy goods vehicle in an area of parkland, golf course and market gardens. In a typical month, the Air Support Unit's helicopters will take an active part in over 450 assignments of all kinds.

The Metropolitan Police Bell 222 helicopters are communications and observation platforms in the sky and for these jobs their equipment must be the best available. Each helicopter can be quickly fitted with the GEC Austria Hele-Teli air-to-ground colour television system. With this, colour video of anything happening on the ground can be quickly relayed back to New Scotland Yard (via a mobile receiver station if necessary) and the film taken can be recorded for later viewing. In addition, the Bells carry a $3\frac{1}{2}$ million candle power Nightsun area illumination searchlight that can light up large areas from 1,000 ft and 'freeze' a suspect in seemingly 'solid' white light; a public address system; stabilized observation binoculars and a Racal TANS F12 computer navigation display system. The TANS is based on the Mk 15 Decca Navigator and the helicopter pilot's position can be displayed as either Decca co-ordinates, latitude/longitude readout, grid reference or bearing and distance to a particular waypoint. If, for example, the pilot needs to go from a position over South London to an incident north-west of London, all he has to do is punch in the map reference on the Decca TANS keyboard and an instant heading to fly and time/distance to run will be displayed on the instrument's screen. Radio communications between air and ground cover all Metropolitan Police channels, Air Traffic Control at Battersea Heliport and Heathrow Airport and of course all UK Aeronautical frequencies.

The helicopter pilots are not policemen trained as aircrew, but civilians seconded from British Caledonian Helicopters, but the observers (there are normally two in each aircraft) are Metropolitan Police officers who have been specially trained for this job (CSE Aviation at Oxford originally trained twenty policemen observers for the Air Support Unit) and they perform normal police duties when not working with the Air Support Group. The police helicopters must observe strict rules when operating over the densely populated London area. They normally fly at heights of between 500 ft and 1,000 ft and when close to the airlanes of Heathrow approach, their maximum altitude is limited to 800 ft. Generally speaking the Bell 222 aircraft only operate outside the Metropolitan Police area when in 'hot pursuit' of a suspect vehicle, and in one case they chased such a vehicle up the M1 motorway as far north as Daventry before police units on the ground could move in and stop the driver.

In America, the police helicopter is a much more familiar sight and even some of the smallest counties usually have access to a police helicopter. The two most popular designs for American law enforcement seem to be the Bell JetRanger and the Hughes 300. A major operator of the JetRanger on police work is the Air Support Division of the Los Angeles City Police Department. LAPD helicopters normally fly two-hour long patrols with a standard operating crew of two, these being a pilot and observer. Unlike some other police departments in America which only recruit trained helicopter crews, usually ex-military pilots, the LAPD trains its own aircrew. The Air Support Division has about thirty pilots on its staff all of whom are all qualified police officers, with at least three years of exemplary ground duty behind them and who have all obtained FAA Commercial Pilots Licences (Helicopter) out of their own pockets or through military service. (Whatever their flying experience most pilots after joining the ASD are given another 200 hours' training on one of the division's five piston-engined Bell 47Gs before flying JetRangers on regular patrols.) The flight observers are mostly ex-patrol car crews and are given on the job training by experienced pilots after selection. In both cases, the unit provides on-going training in police helicopter methods before crews are teamed up for full time air work. Equipment carried by the LAPD JetRangers is basically the same as that of the London Metropolitan Police's Bell 222s, less of course the navigational computer system, the JetRanger being a lighter and simpler aircraft than the twin-engined 222. In Los Angeles, a much larger city than London and more spread out, twin-engined helicopters are not cost effective, there being ample landing space within the city in case of an emergency landing.

On a much smaller scale than the LAPD's Air Support Division, is the Lakewood County Sheriff's single Hughes 300 helicopter. This aircraft is based at Long Beach, California to cover the 35-square-mile area of Artesia, Bellflower, Cerritos, Hawaiian Gardens, Lakewood and Paramount. It takes only three minutes for the helicopter to reach the farthest point of this territory. These six southern California communities contract in with the Los Angeles County Sheriff's department for law enforcement services and share the cost of operating the police helicopter. In this area, the small Hughes is flown by a civilian pilot under contract to the police department, with a deputy sheriff aboard who serves as the observer and law enforcement official. Primary duties for this unit are responding to silent alarms, burglar alarms, prowlers and requests for helicopter assistance.

The Police Bell 222 flying over central London. The helicopter pilot is a civilian from British Caledonian Helicopters, but the observers (there are normally two in each aircraft) are Metropolitan Police officers who have been specially trained for the job.

Above *The Metropolitan Police has eyes in the sky in the shape of the twin-engined Bell 222. Based at Lippitts Hill the aircraft is sometimes fitted with the 'Hele Tele' air to ground colour television system and also carries public address systems and observation binoculars.*

Below *The Enstrom is a popular light helicopter used for general utility duties and pilot training. Seen here is the model 280 Shark. The small wheels on the skid undercarriage are to assist with handling the helicopter when on the ground.*

Oil support operations

The discovery of huge offshore oil reserves in parts of the world such as the Gulf of Mexico, the North Sea and the South China Sea have produced a boom in the civil helicopter industry, for it is only the helicopter than can service and supply the steel and concrete offshore platforms. In order to support these drilling operations, numerous offshore helicopter companies have been formed including Bristow Helicopters, British Airways Helicopters (both UK), Okanagan Helicopters (Canada), Petroleum Helicopters (USA), Bond Helicopters (UK) and Helikopter Service (Norway). Of these, the two largest are Petroleum Helicopters and Bristow Helicopters, with the former being the world's most numerous operator with a fleet of well over 300 aircraft (although the value of the Bristow fleet—packed with Sikorsky S-61Ns and Aérospatiale Super Pumas—is considered to be greater).

Petroleum Helicopters Incorporated had its beginnings in 1949, when seismic crews were fighting their way through a forebidding stretch of Louisiana marsh and swampland. Using ground vehicles proved to be a very slow and arduous way to travel through this type of terrain. Out of desperation it was envisaged that the helicopter might be the solution to their transportation problems and from an initial fleet of three small rotary-wing aircraft, PHI has grown and progressed to the point that it is known throughout the world. Today, PHI serves the oil and gas industry in every phase of its activity, not only in the Gulf of Mexico but from Zaire to the Alaskan North Slopes, crews and helicopters have flown almost every conceivable type of mission in coastal waters and in some of the most remote locations on earth. Current areas of operation include about 600 miles of coastal water along the Gulf of Mexico from Texas to Florida, in California and Colorado, off the North Eastern coast of the United States and in Brazil, Trinidad, Zaire and Saudi Arabia. PHI's large fleet of helicopters includes Aérospatiale SA-330 Pumas, Bell JetRangers and LongRangers, Bell 222s, 212s and 205s, Aérospatiale AS-350 Astars, Sikorsky S-76s and MBB 105s. Principal aircraft of PHI's fleet is the Bell 206 JetRanger.

Very different from the blue skies and calm seas of the Gulf of Mexico is Bristow Helicopters' main area of operation—the North Sea. Here Bristow provides the vital link between the mainland and the platforms up to 300 miles away in a stretch of cold, rough sea well known for its hostile weather. Most of these operations are based in Aberdeen or the Shetland Islands and call for the largest helicopters available. For over-water flying in this rugged environment,

Top left *This civilian Westland Scout served with the Uganda Police Air Wing flying on air supply, reconnaissance survey, communications, air ambulance and general air support operations.*

Centre left *This Scout helicopter served with the Bahrain Police Department in the Gulf.*

Left *The small Hughes 300 utility helicopter is popular for pilot training and law enforcement duties, particularly in the United States where the type is operated by a number of small county sheriffs' departments. The aircraft in this photograph, G-AYNO, served with Air Gregory on charter and training duties.*

twin engines are required as standard and long range operations are now centred on three main types, the Aérospatiale AS-332 Super Puma and the Sikorsky S-76 and S-61N. The Sikorsky S-61N although now an ageing helicopter, is still the major workhorse of the North Sea operators and it is expected to soldier on into the early 1990s. First flown on 7 August 1962, the S-61N seats 26 passengers in a standard airline type seating layout and is operated by a flight crew of two/three. The helicopter is fully amphibious and can be easily identified by its flying-boat hull and twin stabilizing floats, into which the twin-wheel main landing gear retract. Powered by two General Electric CT-58-140-2 turbines each developing 1,500 shp the S-61N has a cruising speed of 150 knots, an operating range of 495 nautical miles and a maximum gross take-off weight of 20,500 lb (9,318 kg). Special equipment fitted for oil support duties includes an automatic flight control system, weather and mapping radar, Decca Navigator or GNS 500 area navigation system, dual VHF radios, single synthesized HF SSB radio, single ADF, dual VOR/ILS, IFR equipment, rescue hoist/winch of 600 lb (273 kg) capacity, engine intakes' ice shield and fuel jettison system. However, technology especially in aviation continues to advance at a rapid rate and newer equipment is now available to offer useful improvements in performance, improvements that will be of considerable benefit to the oilman. Bristow's AS 332 Super Pumas, known as 'Bristow Tigers' and S-76 are a case in point. The AS 332, although externally similar to the original SA 330 Puma, is different in many respects. As well as being fitted with newer and more powerful engines (twin Makila turboshafts) it has a longer nose, single wheel main landing gear, full de-icing capability and more efficient glassfibre composite main and tail rotors. Performance figures for this good-looking helicopter are impressive: a maximum speed of 182 mph (291 km/h), a fast cruise speed of 175 mph (280 km/h), a service ceiling of 15,000 ft (4,600 m) and an operating range of 391 miles (625 km).

The third of these principal oilfield helicopters is the Sikorsky S-76 which was the first helicopter designed by Sikorsky specifically for civil use and Bristow was amongst the first operators to order it. Sikorsky has traditionally concentrated its helicopter construction on large military aircraft, leaving Bell and Aérospatiale to produce machines for the civil market. To expand its share of this lucrative business, Sikorsky designed and built the S-76 as a medium capacity transport helicopter for civil operators. The prototype first took to the air on 13 March 1977 and since then, thanks to its advanced technology and superior performance, cruising speed of 178 knots (via twin Allison 250-C30 turbines of 650 shp), an operating range of 465 nautical miles and a maximum gross take-off weight of 9,700 lb the S-76 has delighted aircrew and passengers alike. Like the S-61N a comprehensive fit of avionics and special equipment to the same level is standard. These three helicopter types together with the Boeing 234 Chinook fill the long-range roles of the oil support operators, but in the more distant future it appears inevitable that even longer range helicopters will be needed to keep pace with oil and gas field developments further and further from the shore.

Above *The Aérospatiale SA 365C Dauphin is a light twin-turbine helicopter used as an executive transport or, as seen here, on oil support duties.*

Below *An Okanagan Bell 214 ST prepares for lift off.*

Above *A float-equipped SE 313B Alouette 2 touches down on the helicopter landing pad of an oil rig.*

Below *This Aérospatiale AS 350D Astar is in service with Petroleum Helicopters Inc, the world's largest helicopter operator, to ferry oil and gas workers to platforms in the Gulf of Mexico, off the Louisiana coast.*

The Westland 30 is in service with a number of civil airlines. The pair seen in this photograph operate with British Airways Helicopters flying to gas rigs in the Southern North Sea.

Above *An Okanagan Sikorsky S-61N on charter to Universal Oil prepares to lift off from the heli deck of an oil support ship.*

Below *Bristow helicopters won a twelve-month contract with the United Kingdom Ministry of Defence to supply three Sikorsky S-61N helicopters for transport duties on the Falkland Islands. The three aircraft were withdrawn from service on the North Sea and shipped to the South Atlantic in August 1983.*

Above *The Sikorsky S-58T is a turbine-engined version of the piston-powered S-58. Seen here in Bristow colours the type is still in worldwide service, though it is no longer used in the North Sea.*

Below *The Aerospatiale AS 332L Super Puma is known by Bristow as the 'Tiger'. This has a long body, enlarged windows, larger liferafts, auto jettison doors and nineteen folding passenger seats. This aircraft is photographed on the flight deck of a North Sea oil platform.*

Below *This Westland Wessex 60 of Bristow helicopters, the commercial version of the military Mk 2 is hard at work in the North Sea, though the type has since been withdrawn from Bristow service. Sykes Aviation of Hurn purchased seven of the aircraft from Bristow's and one of these, G-AYNC, is now employed on a Ministry of Defence contract for infra-red detection trials with military vehicles.*

Right *A Bell 212 twin-engined helicopter of Bristow helicopters.*

Centre right *A Sikorsky S-76 of Bristow helicopters shows its characteristic tail-down hovering attitude.*

Bottom right *An impression of the projected civil EH 101 transport helicopter.*

Appendix
Rotary Wing Reference Table

Type	Engine	Origin	Notes
Aerospace			
Minicopter	90 hp McCulloch piston	USA	Ultralight strap-on one-man helicopter ordered for evaluation by the US Navy and Army.
Aérospatiale			
SE 3101	85 hp Mathis	France	Post-World War 2 French helicopter.
SE 3110	200 hp Salmson 9 NH	France	Two-seat development of the SE 3101.
SO 1221 Djinn	Palouste IV gas turbine	France	First production machine to be powered by compressed air rotor tip-drive jets.
SE 3120	As for 3110	France	Prototype Alouette: this type established several world records in 1953.
SE 3130 Alouette 2	Artouste 2 turbine	France	First flown 12 March 1955.
SA 315 Lama	870 shp Artouste 3B turbine	France	Gained a world height record when it reached a height of 40,820 ft piloted by Jean Boulet on 21 June 1972.

Type	Engine	Origin	Notes
SA 319 Alouette 3	592 shp Astazou XIV turbine	France	Evolved as a larger and more powerful version of the Alouette 2.
Frelon	3 x 800 shp Turmo III B turbines	France	Abandoned in favour of the Super Frelon.
SA 321 Super Frelon	3 x 1,630 shp III C turbines	France	Military transport, heavy civil transport and ASW helicopter.
SA 330 Puma	2 x 1,328 shp Turmo IIIC 4 turbines	France/UK	A twin-engined medium-sized transport helicopter produced jointly with Westland Helicopters and CNA Romania.
AS 332 Super Puma	2 x 1,755 shp Makila IA turbines	France	Improved version of the SA 330.
SA 341/2 Gazelle	592 shp Astazou IIIA turbine	France/UK	Light military and civil machine.
349-2	Astazou 14 turbine	France	Experimental version of the Gazelle.
AS 350 Ecureuil	641 shp Arriel turbine	France	Replacing the Alouette series; the Squirrel is a light general purpose helicopter.
AS 355 Ecureuil 2	2 x 422 shp Allison turbines	France	Twin-engined version of the Squirrel.
SA 360 Dauphin	1,050 shp Astazou turbine	France	General purpose machine with a 'Fenestron' tail rotor.
SA 365 Dauphin 2	2 x 650 shp Arriel turbines	France	Civil and military twin-engined version of the SA 360.

Aerotechnia

Type	Engine	Origin	Notes
AC 12	168 hp 0-360-B2A Lycoming piston	Spain	Light three-seat helicopter first flown on 20 July 1956.
AC 14	360 shp Artouste IIB turbine	Spain	Light five-seat helicopter first flown on 16 July 1957.

Type	Engine	Origin	Notes
Agusta			
AZ 101G	3 x 1, 250 shp Gnome turbines	Italy	Three-engined heavy-duty helicopter in the same class as the French Super Frelon.
A 102	600 shp 51H4-R 1340 Pratt & Whitney turbine	Italy	Utility transport based on the Bell Model 48.
A 104	140 hp MUA-140V piston	Italy	Two-seat light general purpose helicopter first flown in December 1960.
A 105	Astazou turbine	Italy	Predecessor of the A 106.
A 106	354 shp Augusta TM 251 turbine	Italy	Single-seat ASW helicopter.
A 109	2 x 420 shp 250 C20 B Allison turbines	Italy	Twin-engined general purpose military and civil helicopter.
A 129 Mongoose	2 x 915 shp Gem 2 turbines	Italy	Anti-tank helicopter for the Italian Army.
47	270 hp Lycoming TVO 435 B1A piston	Italy	Licence-built version of the Bell 47.
204	Rolls-Royce Gnome H1200 or GE T 58 turbine	Italy	Licence-built version of the Bell UH-1B. ASW AS 204 locally built.
205	1,400 shp Lycoming T531A turbine	Italy	Licence-built version of the Bell UH-1D.
206	400 shp Allison 250 C20 turbine	Italy	Licence-built version of the Bell 206 JetRanger.
212	One Pratt & Whitney PT6T Twin Pac turbine	Italy	Licence-built version of the Bell 212. ASW AS 212 is locally built.
412	1,308 shp PT6T-3B Pratt & Whitney Twin Pac turbine	Italy	Licence-built version of the Bell 412.

Type	Engine	Origin	Notes
ASH 3D/H	2 x 1,400 shp T58 GE 5 General Electric turbines	Italy	Licence-built version of the Sikorsky Sea King.
AS 61 N1	2 x 1,400 shp T58 GE 5 General Electric turbines	Italy	Licence-developed version of the Sikorsky S-61.
AS 61 R	2 x 1,500 shp T58 GE 5 General Electric turbines	Italy	Licence-built version of the Sikorsky HH-3F.
EMB CH 47	2 x 3,750 shp T55 L 11C Lycoming turbines	Italy	Licence-built version of the Boeing Vertol CH 47 Chinook.

Airmaster

H2 B1	100 hp Rolls-Royce 0200A Continental	UK	Small two-seater with two-blade rigid all-metal main rotor

American

XH-26 Jet Jeep	2 x 35 lb thrust pulsejets	USA	Small tip-driven helicopter

Avro

Rota	140 hp Armstrong Siddeley Genet Major	UK	First rotary wing to serve with the RAF.

Avian

2/180B	180 hp 036A Lycoming piston	Canada	Two/three-seat wingless gyroplane with vertical take-off and landing capability first flown in 1960.

Barnet

J3M	65 hp Continental	USA	Ultralight single-seat gyroplane designed for home construction.

Bell

30	160 hp Franklin piston	USA	First flown in early 1943 and employing the stabilizing bar common to all Bell helicopters.
47	200 hp Franklin 6V4 200 C32 piston	USA	Commercial production version of the Model 30. The

Type	*Engine*	*Origin*	*Notes*
			first commercial certificate was granted to the Model 47 on 8 March 1946. It was in production with Bell until 1974 and with Agusta until 1976.
47 J	305 hp Lycoming VO 540 B1B piston	USA	Covered fuselage version of the Bell 47 known as the Ranger.
HSL-1	2,400 hp Pratt & Whitney Double Wasp Radial piston	USA	Twin-rotor helicopter used on ASW duties with the US Navy.
XH-40	700 shp Lycoming T53 turbine	USA	Prototype Huey for the US Army first flown on 22 October 1956.
204/205 Huey	Various engine fits	USA	Utility helicopter in worldwide civil and military use.
OH-4A	Allison turbine	USA	Forerunner of the Bell OH-58/206 JetRanger first flown on 8 December 1962.
OH-13X	260 hp Lycoming TVO 435	USA	The Sioux Scout was the prototype of the Cobra gunship and first flew in September 1963.
206	420 shp Allison 250-C20B turbine	USA	Military and civil utility helicopter. Loser in the LOH contest of 1962 to Hughes 'Cayuse' it went on to serve in large numbers with the US Armed Forces.
206L	420 shp Allison 250-C20B turbine	USA	Stretched version of the Bell 206 JetRanger.

Type	Engine	Origin	Notes
OH-58	As for Bell 206 and 206 L	USA	US Army version of the Bell 206: US Navy has the TH-57A Sea Ranger.
209	1,400 shp Lycoming T53 13 turbine (AH-1G)	USA	The Huey Cobra gunship first flown on 7 September 1965.
309	2,050 shp Lycoming T55 L7C turbine	USA	King Cobra is a further development model of the 209.
AH-1T	2 x General Electric T 700-401 turbines	USA	USMC version of the Bell 209 known as the Sea Cobra.
YAH-63	2 x 1,536 shp GET-700 turbines	USA	Unsuccessful entry in the US Army's AAH contest.
ACAP	2 x 615 shp Lycoming 101 650C2 turbines	USA	Research helicopter based on the Bell 222 for Advanced Composite Airframe Program.
214	2 x 1,625 shp CT-72A GE turbines	USA	Military and civil utility helicopter.
222	2 x 675 shp Lycoming 101 650 C2 turbines	USA	Twin-engined commercial light helicopter.
301/XV-15	2 x 1,550 shp Lycoming LTC 1K 4K turbines	USA	Tilt rotor research aircraft under contract to the US Army and NASA.
Texas-Ranger	420 shp Allison turbine	USA	Military version of the Bell 206 L.

Bensen

B8M	72 hp 4318 McCulloch piston	USA	Ultralight single seat gyrocopter.

Berger

BX 110	130 hp Wankel piston	Swiss	Two-seat light helicopter.

Boeing Vertol

CH-47	2 x 3,750 shp	USA	The standard

Type	Engine	Origin	Notes
Chinook	Lycoming T55 L11C turbines		medium lift helicopter of the US Army.
234 Chinook	2 x 3,750 shp T-55 Lycoming turbines	USA	Civil version of the CH-47 Chinook.
YUH-61A	2 x 1,500 shp GE T 700 turbines	USA	Unsuccessful entry in the US Army's (UTTAS) contest.
107	2 x 1,250 shp GE CT 58 110 1 turbines	USA	Twin-rotor military and civil transport helicopter known as the Sea Knight in US Navy and Marines service.
XCH-62	3 x 8,079 shp Allison T701 turbines	USA	Experimental tandem-rotor heavy lift helicopter.

Bond

Skymaster	90 hp Revmaster piston	USA	Single-seat gyroplane.

Brantly-Hynes

B2	180 hp Lycoming IVO 360 A1A piston	USA	Two-seat light helicopter with a unique rotor design.
305	305 hp Lycoming IVO 540 A1A piston	USA	Five-seat version of the Model B2.

Bratukhin

Omega	2 x 500 hp Ivchenko A1 26 GR Seven Cylinder piston radials.	USSR	Experimental twin lateral rotored helicopter of 1943.

Breguet-Dorand

Gyroplane-Laboratoire	350 hp 9Q Hispano radial piston	France	Early co-axial rotor helicopter.

Breguet-Richet

1 & 2	40/45 hp Antoinette piston	France	Early experimental helicopter.

Bristol

171 Sycamore	550 hp Alvis Leonides 173 piston	UK	Light civil and military helicopter.
173	2 x 550 hp nine-cylinder Alvis Leonides pistons	UK	Twin-rotor helicopter.

Type	Engine	Origin	Notes
Buhl			
Autogyro	165 hp Continental piston	USA	Two-seat autogyro designed for observation and photographic work.
Campbell			
Cricket	72 hp converted Volkswagen engine	UK	Single-seat light autogyro with small fuselage nacelle, open cockpit and tricycle landing gear.
Cicare			
CK 1	190-200 hp of an unknown type	Argentina	Lightweight training helicopter.
Cierva			
C6	110 hp Le Rhône rotary piston	UK	Autogyro built on the fuselage of an Avro 504K.
C8L Mk 2	200 hp Armstrong Siddeley Lynx piston	UK	This machine was the first rotorcraft to fly across the English Channel on 18 September 1928.
W9	1,205 hp DH Gipsy V1 piston	UK	Experimental helicopter of 1946 used jet exhaust in place of tail rotor.
W 11 Air Horse	1,620 hp Rolls-Royce Merlin 24 piston	UK	Single piston-engined three-rotored helicopter; the largest in the world when it flew in December 1948.
Grasshopper	2 x 210 hp Continental TS10 360A pistons	UK	Co-axial contra-rotating four-seat commercial light helicopter.
Continental-Copters			
Tomcat	270 hp Lycoming TVO 435 B1A piston	USA	Single-seat agricultural conversion of the basic Bell 47.

Type	Engine	Origin	Notes
Cornu			
Helicopter	24 hp Antoinette piston	France	First early helicopter to lift off and complee a free flight in 1907.
CSIR			
Sara 3	180 hp Lycoming 036A piston	South Africa	Two-seat twin-boom experimental autogyro first flown on 30 November 1972.
Dornier			
DO 32E	90 shp BMW 601 2L turbine	W. Germany	Ultralight helicopter first flown on 29 June 1962.
Ekstrom			
Humlan 2	90 hp McCulloch AF100-X3 piston	Sweden	Single-seat autogyro first flown in June 1973.
Ellehammer			
Helio	36 hp Ellehammer air cooled piston	Denmark	Early Danish helicopter of around 1912.
Enstrom			
F 28	205 hp Lycoming HIO 360 C1B piston	USA	Three-seat light utility helicopter.
280 F	225 hp Lycoming HIO 360 fuel injected F1AD piston	USA	The Shark, an improved version of the F 28; 280 FX is the turbine version.
Fairchild-Hiller			
FH 1100	317 shp Allison 250 C18 turbine	USA	Five-seat light turbine powered helicopter.
Fairey			
Gyrodyne	525 hp Leonides piston	UK	Experimental compound helicopter, forerunner of the Rotordyne.

Type	*Engine*	*Origin*	*Notes*
Rotordyne	2 x 2,8000 shp Napier turboprops	UK	Experimental commercial compound helicopter with turboprop engines mounted on stub wings and tip drive.

Flettner

FI 184	150 hp radial piston	Germany	Single-seat autogyro first flown in 1935.
FI 185	140 hp Siemens Halske piston	Germany	Experimental helicopter fitted with two outrigger propellers for forward or reverse thrust.
FL 265	150 hp Bramo SH14 A piston	Germany	Single-seat experimental helicopter.
FL 282	150 hp Bramo SH14 A piston	Germany	Saw active duty with the German armed forces during World War 2.

Focke Achgelis

FA 223	1,000 hp Bramo 323 Q3 piston	Germany	World War 2 German transport helicopter.
FA 226	840 hp Bramo piston	Germany	Commercial helicopter project never completed.

Focke Wulf

Fw 61	160 hp Bramo piston	Germany	Lateral rotor helicopter.

Fuji Bell

204	Rolls-Royce Gnome H1200 or Lycoming T53 or GE T58 turbine	Japan	Licence-built version of the Bell 204.

HAL

ALH	1,318 shp Astazou turbine	India	Under joint development with MBB.

Type	Engine	Origin	Notes
Helicop Jet			
Helo	500 hp Astazou Turbo generator	France	Four/five-seat helicopter powered by cold jet tip drive.
Heligyro			
Phoenix	220 hp Victor	USA	Light helicopter driven by tip-mounted cold jets and intended for amateur construction.
Hiller			
360	178 hp Franklin piston	USA	Three-seat light helicopter.
UH-12/ H-23	178 hp Franklin	USA	Three-seat helicopter in widespread use.
OH-5A/ 1100	250 shp Allison T63 turbine	USA	Unsuccessful entry for the US Army LOH contest.
1099	500 shp PT6 B 3 Pratt & Whitney turbine	USA	Six-seat utility helicopter.
Hollman			
HA 2M	130 hp Franklin sport piston	USA	Two-seat twin-boom light autogyro first flown in October 1974.
Hoppicopter			
Helicopter	20 hp piston	USA	One man back-mounted helicopter intended to carry infantry soldiers into action.
Hughes			
XH-17	2 x General Electric turbojets	USA	Giant heavy lift helicopter powered by compressed air blade-tip pressure jets.
500C	317 shp Allison turbine	USA	Light five-seat helicopter.
500D	420 shp Allison turbine	USA	Uprated version of the 500C; 500E has redesigned cabin/ nose.

Type	Engine	Origin	Notes
530F	650 shp Allison turbine	USA	For hot/high operations.
OH-6A	317 shp Allison turbine	USA	Cayuse scout and light observation helicopter of the US Army.
NOTAR	317 shp Allison turbine	USA	Modified OH-6A where the tail rotor has been replaced with a variable gas exhaust fan.
500MD	420 shp Allison turbine	USA	Light anti-tank helicopter; ASW version available.
530MG	650 shp Allison turbine	USA	Light attack helicopter.
AH-64A	2 x 1,536 shp T700 General Electric turbines	USA	Apache is the latest US Army attack helicopter.

Hughes/Schweitzer

Type	Engine	Origin	Notes
300/ TH-55A	190 hp Lycoming 360 piston	USA	Light training helicopter.

Kaman

Type	Engine	Origin	Notes
HTK 1	Twin turbine	USA	Early twin-rotor machine first flown on 26 March 1954.
H-43 Huskie	Lycoming T53 Free turbine	USA	Twin intermeshing rotor light helicopter.
SH-2	2 x 1,350 shp General Electric turbines	USA	The Seasprite was the standard US small ship's helicopter. First flown on 2 July 1959, it is still in production.

Kamov

Type	Engine	Origin	Notes
Ka-15 Hen	255 hp Ivchenko A1 14 piston	USSR	General purpose utility helicopter.
Ka-18 Hog	255 hp Ivchenko A1 14 V piston	USSR	Four-seat contra-rotating military helicopter.
Ka-20 Harp	As for Ka-25	USSR	Prototype ASW helicopter.

Type	Engine	Origin	Notes
Ka-22 Hoop	2 x 5,500 shp D25V Soloviev turbines	USSR	Large lateral-rotor compound helicopter.
Ka-25 Hormone	2 x 900 shp Glushenkov GTD turbines	USSR	Ship-based ASW, SAR and general duties helicopter.
Ka-25K	As for KA-25	USSR	Commercial version of the Ka-25.
Ka-26 Hoodlum	2 x 325 hp Vedeneev M 14V 26 radial pistons	USSR	Military and civil general purpose light helicopter.
Kawasaki			
KH-4	270 hp Lycoming TVO D1A piston	Japan	Four-seat light helicopter based on the Bell 47.
KHR-1	As for KH-4	Japan	KH-4 fitted with rigid three-blade rotor.
KV-107	2 x 1,250 shp General Electric CT 58 110 1 turbines	Japan	Licence-built version of the Boeing Vertol 107.
Kellet			
KD 1	225 hp Jacob L4MA piston	USA	Single-seat autogyro operated by Eastern Airlines on a mail contract in 1939.
K3	165 hp Continental piston	USA	Two-seat autogyro with stub wings.
KG 1A	165 hp Jacob piston	USA	Military version of the Kellet KD 1.
Lockheed			
AH-56A Cheyenne	General Electric T64-GE-16 3,925 shp turbine	USA	Two-seat advanced anti-tank and gunship helicopter.
CL-595	500 shp Pratt & Whitney T74 turbine	USA	Research helicopter.
MBB			
105	2 x 420 shp Allison turbines	FDR	Light civil helicopter first flown on 16 February 1967.
105 P	As for MBB 105	FDR	Anti-tank helicopter in service with the West German Army.

Type	Engine	Origin	Notes
MBB/Kawasaki			
BK 117	2 x 650 shp Lycoming LTS 101 turbines	FDR/Japan	Twin-engined light helicopter.
Meger			
Helistar	200 hp Lycoming HIO 360 C1A piston	USA	High performance helicopter developed from Enstrom F-28
Mil			
Mi-1 Hare	575 hp Ivchenko A1 26 radial piston	USSR	Light general and utility helicopter.
Mi-2 Hoplite	2 x 450 shp Isotov GTD-350 turbines	USSR	Multi-role utility helicopter.
Mi-4 Hound	1,700 hp Shvetsov 82V piston	USSR	Multi-role transport and ASW helicopter.
Mi-6 Hook	2 x 5,500 shp Soloviev D25 V turbines	USSR	Heavy transport helicopter.
Mi-8 Hip	2 x 1,700 shp Isotov TV 2 117A turbines	USSR	General transport, armed assault and electronic warfare helicopter.
Mi-10 Harke	2 x 5,500 shp Soloviev D25V turbines	USSR	Heavy lift flying crane.
Mi-10 K Harke	As for Mi-10	USSR	Utility version of Mi-10.
Mi-12 Homer	4 x 6,500 shp Soloviev D25 VF turbines	USSR	Heavy transport helicopter.
Mi-14 Haze	2 x 2,200 shp Isotov TV2-117A turbines	USSR	Land-based ASW helicopter in service with the Soviet Navy.
Mi-17 Hip-H	2 x 1,900 shp Isotov 117-MT turbines	USSR	Developed from the Mi-8.
Mi-24 Hind	2 x 2,200 shp Isotov TV2-117A turbines	USSR	Armed assault and anti-tank helicopter.
Mi-26 Halo	2 x 11,400 shp Lotarev D-136 turbines	USSR	Largest production helicopter in the world.
Oemichen			
No 2	180 hp Gnome rotary piston	France	Early helicopter from the 1920s.

Type	Engine	Origin	Notes
Pescara			
No 3	180 hp Hispano-Suiza piston	Spain	Built in 1923, by 1924 the No 3 was making flights of ten minutes duration.
Phillips			
Mk 1	145 hp Rolls-Royce Continental piston	Australia	Two-seat light utility helicopter.
Piasecki			
Hup	525 hp Continental R-975-34 piston	USA	US Navy SAR helicopter.
HRP-1 Rescuer	600 hp Pratt & Whitney R-1340-AN-1 piston	USA	Tandem-rotor transport and utility helicopter.
H-21 Shawnee	1,425 hp Wright R1820 103 Cyclone piston	USA	Twin-rotor transport helicopter.
Pathfinder	1,250 shp T58 GE 5 General Electric turbine	USA	Research compound helicopter first flown on 21 February 1962.
Pitcairn			
PA-34	420 hp Wright R975-EQ radial piston	USA	Experimental military autogyro designated XOP-2 by the US Navy.
Rotorcraft			
Grasshopper	2 x 100 hp Rolls-Royce Continental pistons	UK	Two-seat light utility helicopter first flown in March 1962.
Rotodyne			
	2 x 2,800 bhp Napier turboprops	UK	Experimental commercial compound helicopter with turboprop engines mounted on stub wings and tip drive
Rotorway			
Scorpion	133 hp Rotorway piston	USA	Single-seat light helicopter for amateur construction.
Scheutzow			
Bee	180 hp IVO-360-A11A Lycoming piston	USA	Light utility two-seat helicopter first flown in 1966.

Type	Engine	Origin	Notes
Siai Marchetti			
SV-20A	2 x 900 shp UALC PT6C 30 turbines	Italy	Twin-engined compound helicopter.
Sikorsky			
VS-300	90 hp Franklin piston	USA	World's first practical helicopter, first flown on 14 September 1939.
R-4	180 hp Warner R 550 1 Super Scarab piston	USA	Early military helicopter.
R-5	As for R-4	USA	Further version of the R-4 designated HO2S-1 in US Navy service.
R-6 Hoverfly 2	245 hp Franklin 0 405 9 piston	USA	Light helicopter.
S-51	450 hp R 985 4B Pratt & Whitney Wasp junior piston	USA	Four-seat light helicopter.
S-55 Chickasaw	600 hp R 1340 57 Pratt & Whitney Wasp piston	USA	General purpose helicopter first flown 10 November 1949.
S-56 Mojave	2 x 1,900 hp R 2800 50 Double Wasp pistons	USA	Heavy assault transport first flown 18 December 1953.
S-58 Choctaw/ Seabat	1,525 hp Wright Cyclone R 1820 84 piston	USA	Utility transport, ASW, SAR and general purpose helicopter first flown on 8 March 1954.
S-58T	Pratt & Whitney PT6T Twin Pac turbine	USA	Turbine-powered utility helicopter.
S-61	2 x General Electric T58 turbines	USA	Twin-engined amphibious naval helicopter first flown on 11 March 1959.
SH-3D/H Sea King	2 x General Electric 1,400 shp T58 GE 10 turbines	USA	Naval ASW helicopter; licence production by Agusta, Mitsubishi and Westland.

Type	*Engine*	*Origin*	*Notes*
S-61N	2 x General Electric CT 58 140 2 1,500 shp turbines	USA	Commercial helicopter for offshore work.
S-61L	As for S-61N	USA	All-weather commercial version of the S-61N.
S-61R Jolly Green Giant	2 x General Electric 1,500 shp T58 GE 5 turbines	USA	Medium utility and SAR aircraft, first helicopter to fly non-stop across the North Atlantic.
S-62 Sea Guard	1,250 shp CT58-G-8 General Electric turbine	USA	Single-engined civil and military helicopter.
S-64 Tarhe	2 x 4,500 shp Pratt & Whitney T73 P1 turbines	USA	Heavy-lift crane helicopter.
S-65 Sea Stallion	2 x 3,925 shp General Electric T64 GE 413 turbines	USA	Heavy transport and assault helicopter first flown on 14 October 1964.
S-65E Super-Stallion	3 x 4,380 shp General Electric T64 GE 415 turbines	USA	Three-engined development of the S-65.
S-67 Blackhawk	2 x 1,500 shp General Electric T58 GE 5 turbines	USA	Experimental gunship helicopter.
S-69 ABC	Pratt & Whitney PT 6T turbo twin pac with two Pratt & Whitney J 60 auxiliary turbojets	USA	The advancing blade concept aircraft capable of 300 knots.
S-70A Blackhawk	2 x 1,543 shp General Electric T700 GE-700 turbines.	USA	Assault and transport helicopter.
S-70B/L Seahawk	As for S70A	USA	Shipborne ASW helicopter; LAMPS III air vehicle for US Navy.
S-70C	As for S-70A	USA	Commercial version of Blackhawk.

Type	Engine	Origin	Notes
S-70D Night Hawk	As for S-70A	USA	To meet a USAF requirement for a combat rescue helicopter.
S-72 RSRA	2 x 1,400 shp General Electric T58 GE 5 turbines (plus 2 x General Electric TF 34 GE 2 turbofans)	USA	High-speed multi-purpose research helicopter.
S-76	2 x 650 shp Allison 250 C30 turbines	USA	General purpose commercial helicopter first flown on 13 March 1977.
H-76B Eagle	Pratt & Whitney PT6T Twin Pac	USA	Combat support version of the S-76.
Silvercraft			
SH-4	235 hp Franklin 6A 350 D1 A piston	Italy	Light utility and general agricultural helicopter first flown in March 1955.
Spitfire			
Spitfire Mk 1	420 shp Allison 250 C20 B turbine	USA	Lightweight three-seat helicopter; based on Enstrom F-28.
TsAGI			
2-EA	230 hp Gnome Rhone Titan radial piston	USSR	Soviet two-place tandem autogyro of 1931.
A-4	300 hp M 26 radial piston	USSR	The first Soviet rotary-winged aircraft to enter service, in 1934.
A-12	640 hp Wright Cyclone F 3 radial piston	USSR	A single-seat autogyro.
Wagner			
Sky Trac	260 hp Franklin 6 AS 335 B piston	FDR	Light helicopter with co-axial contra-rotating rotors.
Wallis			
WA-116	72 hp McCulloch piston	UK	Record-holding small single-seat light autogyro.

Type	Engine	Origin	Notes
Westermayer			
WE04	70 hp Volkswagen piston	Austria	Single-seat light autogyro designed for amateur construction.
Westland			
Dragonfly	550 hp Alvis Leonides piston	UK	Licence-built version of the Sikorsky S-51.
Widgeon	500 hp Alvis Leonides 521 piston	UK	Developed from the Dragonfly.
Westminster	2 x 2,800 shp Napier Eland turbines	UK	Heavy lift helicopter funded by Westlands.
Belvedere	2 x 1,650 shp Napier Gazelle turbines	UK	Twin-rotor RAF tactical transport helicopter.
Skeeter	200 hp DH Gipsy Major piston	UK	Light observation and training helicopter.
Whirlwind Series 1	600 hp Wasp Pratt & Whitney R1340-40 piston	UK	Licence-built version of the Sikorsky S-55.
Whirlwind Series 2	750 hp Alvis Leonides de-rated Major piston	UK	RAF transport version.
Whirlwind Series 3	1,050 shp Rolls-Royce Gnome turbine	UK	Trooping, SAR and VIP version.
Wessex HAS Mk 1	1,450 shp Napier Gazelle 161 turbine	UK	Licence-built commando/ASW version of the Sikorsky S-58.
Wessex HC Mk 2	2 x 1,350 shp Bristol Siddeley Gnome turbines	UK	Troop and transport helicopter.
Wessex HAS Mk 3	1,600 shp Napier Gazelle 165 turbine	UK	Royal Navy ASW helicopter.
Wessex HU Mk 5	2 x 1,250 shp Rolls-Royce Gnome turbines	UK	Commando assault helicopter.
Wessex Mk 60	2 x 1,350 shp Rolls-Royce Gnome turbines	UK	Commercial version of the Mk 5.

Type	Engine	Origin	Notes
Sioux	270 hp Lycoming piston	UK	Licence-built version of Bell 47.
Scout	685 shp Nimbus 101 or 102 turbine	UK	A five-seat battlefield utility helicopter.
Wasp	710 shp Nimbus turbine	UK	Small ship's helicopter replaced by the Lynx.
Sea King	2 x 1,500 shp Rolls-Royce Gnome H-1400 1 turbines	UK	Licence-built version of the Sikorsky S-61.
Sea King/ Commando	As for Sea King	UK	Tactical transport and support helicopter.
606	2 x Rolls-Royce Gem turbines	UK	A proposed twelve-seat civil version of the Lynx.
30 Series 100	2 x 1,135 shp Rolls-Royce Gem 41 turbines	UK	Multi-role utility or passenger helicopter.
30 Series 100-60	2 x 1,260 shp Rolls-Royce Gem 60 turbines	UK	Improved engine performance.
30 Series 200	2 x 1,712 shp General Electric CT 7 2B turbines	UK	Improved version.
Lynx	2 x 1,120 shp Rolls-Royce Gem 41-1 turbines	UK	Light battlefield or ASW helicopter.
Lynx-3	2 x 1,115 shp Rolls-Royce Gem 60 turbines	UK	Combat support version of the Lynx.
WHE			
Airbuggy	75 hp Volkswagen piston	UK	Light gyroplane fitted with a semi-rigid teetering rotor and first flown on 1 February 1973.
Yakovlev			
Yak-24 Horse	2 x 1,700 hp Shvetsov pistons	USSR	Tandem-rotor tactical transport helicopter.

★ Note The many marks and variants of engines decree that the powerplants listed in this table are the major or initial production types.

Glossary

Basic helicopter aerodynamics

Advancing blade   That half of the rotor disc in which the rotor blade is travelling in the same direction as the movement of the aircraft.

Airfoil   A curved surface designed to produce lift when air is passed over it.

Airframe   The airframe is the basic body of the helicopter including the doors, seats, cabin, canopy, landing gear and so on.

Angle of attack   The angle as measured between the chord of the rotor blade or airfoil and the relative wind.

Angle of incidence   Sometimes used in the same sense as angle of attack.

Articulated rotor   A rotor disc system where the individual blades are free to flap, drag and feather.

Autogyro   Not a true helicopter, the autogyro depends on its movement through the air rather than direct engine power to keep its rotor system turning and sustain flight.

Autorotation   A non-powered flight condition in which the helicopter descends with its rotor system being driven by the action of the relative wind only, a controlled descent can be made because the rotors are still producing lift. In an autorotational descent the air enters the rotor system from below rather than from above as in powered flight.

Axial flow   The flow of air through the rotor system which is normal to the rotors' tip path plane.

Axis of rotation   An imaginary line which intersects a point around which a body rotates, normal to its plane of rotation.

Bernoullis Theorem   Lift forces are produced because of the difference in the air pressure above and below the airfoil or rotor blade when it is in motion. Thus Bernoullis Theorem states: 'as the velocity increases, pressure decreases'.

Blade   The airfoil surface of a helicopter used to produce lift.

Blade damper   A device installed on the vertical hinge to dampen rotor blade oscillation around the hinge.

Blade loading   The load placed on the rotor blades determined by dividing the gross weight of the helicopter by the total area of all the rotor blades.

Centre of gravity   An imaginary point on the body of the helicopter where the resultant of all weight forces may be considered to be concentrated.

Centrifugal force   A force created by the tendency of the body to follow a straight path against the force which causes it to move in a curve, resulting in a pull away from the axis of rotation.

Chord   An imaginary line passing through the leading and trailing edges of an airfoil.

Clutch   The 'Sprag' clutch allows the rotor system to disengage from the engine and freewheel, thus permitting autorotation.

Co-axial rotor system   A co-axial rotor system consists of two rotor systems mounted atop one another which rotate in opposite directions, thus eliminating torque.

Collective pitch lever   The pilot's control which increases or decreases the pitch of all main rotor blades equally and simultaneously.

Compound helicopter   A compound helicopter combines the rotary and fixed-wing aircraft and may be fitted with fixed wings and auxiliary turbofan or jet engines.

Coning   The tendency of helicopter blades to flex upward when they are lifting the weight of the aircraft. The gross weight of the helicopter and the rotor rpm will determine the coning angle.

Contra-rotating rotor system   A tandem-rotored helicopter in which the individual rotor systems rotate in opposite directions.

Coriolis effect The tendency of a mass to increase or decrease its angular velocity when its radius of rotation is increased or decreased.

Cyclic pitch stick   The pilots control equivalent to the control stick of a fixed-wing aeroplane, which changes the pitch of the rotor blades individually during a complete revolution to control the tilt of the rotor disc and thus the direction and velocity of the helicopter's flight path.

Delta hinge   The hinge parallel to the plane of rotation which lets the rotor blades equalize lift between the advancing and retreating blades.

Density altitude   Pressure altitude corrected for humidity and temperature.

Disc area   The area swept by the blades of the helicopter rotor system.

Disc loading   The ratio of gross helicopter weight to rotor disc area.

Dissymmetry of lift   The unequal lift across a helicopter rotor disc arising from the difference in the velocity of the air passing over the advancing and retreating rotor blades of the rotor disc area.

Engine (powerplant)   The engine be it piston or turbine, delivers power to the transmission which in turn powers the main lifting rotor system and the anti-torque tail rotor.

Feathering action   The changing of the pitch angle of the rotor blades periodically by rotating them about their feathering axis.

Feathering axis   The axis about which the angle of pitch of the individual rotor blade is varied.

Flapping   The vertical movement of an individual rotor blade about a delta hinge.

Flexible blade   A rotor system where the individual blades have no hinges or pivots, the blades themselves are flexible.

Free-wheeling unit   See Sprag clutch.

Friction locks   Adjusts pressures of individual controls to pilot's requirements and also provides positive locking of cyclic and throttle controls in any position.

Fuel flow indicator   Indicates the flow of aviation fuel.

Gearbox (90 degree)   The gearbox at right angles or 90 degrees to the tail rotor through which power is supplied via the main drive shaft.

Ground effect   The cushion of air beneath the rotor system of a hovering helicopter.

Ground resonance   A series of ground shocks which can unbalance the rotor head. Usually encountered after a rough or very uneven landing in certain types of helicopters the phenomenon can result in the total destruction of the aircraft in a very short space of time.

Gyroplane   Another name for a light autogyro.

Gyroscopic precession   When a force is applied to a spinning body the resultant action takes place 90 degrees later in the plane of rotation.

Helicopter   A rotary-winged aircraft which produces lift by means of a powered rotor system.

Hovering   Maintaining a fixed position over a given point on the ground at some height above the surface.

Hovering out of ground effect   Hovering at a height above the surface at which no additional lift is obtained from ground effect.

Impeller   A device mounted on top of the helicopter's engine compartment to 'impel' cooling air.

Instruments   Information reference for the helicopter pilot: height, speed, fuel flow, rotor rpm, engine rpm, altitude and so on.

Intermeshing rotor system   A contra-rotating rotor system in which the rotor blades intermesh.

Landing gear   Skid, wheel or float system that supports the helicopter's weight whilst on the ground.

Landing light   A powerful light in the nose of the helicopter used to light up an area of ground prior to landing at night.

Lateral rotors   Rotors mounted at equal distances to the left and right of the helicopter body.

Lead lag   The motion of rotor blades of an articulated rotor system about their hinge pins.

Lift   The force needed to overcome weight. See Bernoullis Theorem.

Longitudinal axis   An imaginary straight line passing through a helicopter from nose to tail. Movement about this axis is 'rolling'.

Pitch angle   The angle between the chord line of the rotor blade and the reference plane of the main rotor hub.

Retreating blade tip stall   A condition which occurs to the retreating blade at high forward speeds.

Reverse flow effect   An area of the rotor disc in which the rotor blade is 'backing' with respect to the surrounding air.

Rigid rotor Rotor blades fixed to the main rotor hub that can feather, but not drag or flap.

Rotor The flight of a helicopter is governed by the angle of pitch of the main rotor blades as they sweep through the air. If the helicopter climbs or descends, the pitch of all the rotor blades is changed at the same time and to the same degree. To climb, the pitch of the rotor blade is increased, to descend the pitch on the blade is decreased. Because all the rotor blades are acting simultaneously or collectively, this is known as collective pitch. For forward, backward or sideways flight an additional change of pitch is required. By this means the pitch of each rotor blade increases at the same selected point in its rotation. This is known as cyclic pitch. These two forms of rotor blade pitch give the helicopter its unique flying ability.

Rotor brake Provides smooth, gradual engagement or disengagement of the helicopter's rotor system.

Rotorcraft A name for an aircraft which flies by means of a rotor system.

Semi-rigid rotor Rotor system in which the individual blades are fastened to the main hub but can flap and feather.

Settling with power May be caused by a vertical descent, under power with a low or zero forward airspeed.

Span The maximum measured distance on the rotor blade centre line from root to tip.

Slip The flight of a helicopter when its direction is not in line with its longitudinal axis.

Solidity ratio The ratio of total blade area to total disc area.

Stall A condition of flight where the angle of attack is increased until the streamlined flow of air over the rotor blade is broken by eddies and the blade stalls and loses lift.

Swashplate An assembly around the hub for conveying to the rotor blades a cyclic pitch change.

Synchropter A helicopter with an intermeshing rotor system.

Tail rotor A small rotor mounted at the tail of the helicopter to counter the torque effect of the main rotor system.

Tandem rotor system Contra-rotating rotor system employed on certain helicopters, where the rotors are mounted fore and aft of the main helicopter body; no tail or anti-torque rotor is necessary.

Throttle Used for start up and other rpm adjustments whilst in flight.

Thrust The force that overcomes drag, and powers the helicopter in the desired direction.

Tip path plane The plane along which the blade tips travel when rotating.

Tip speed The speed of the rotor at its tip.

Tip speed ratio The ratio between the speed of the rotor blade tips and the forward speed of the helicopter.

Tracking Used to check the blade tips are rotating in a common plane.

Translating tendency A single-rotor helicopter has a tendency to drift to the right whilst hovering due to the thrust provided by the anti-torque or tail rotor.

Translational lift   The additional lift obtained through airspeed when transitioning from the hover in to forward flight.

Transmission   The transmission supplies power from the engine to the main rotor blades.

Transverse flow effect   As the relative wind approaches the rotor disc, the air that is to enter the rear portion of the disc will have been accelerated. This accelerated air causes differential lift which results in the retreating rotor blade flapping upward.

Trim   Used to compensate pilot control pressures caused by variable flying conditions.

Twist   Individual rotor blades usually have a twist built in along their span, giving an even distribution of lift over the complete rotor blade.

Key to abbreviations

The following abbreviations are common to rotary wing aviation and may prove useful to the reader.

AAC   Army Air Corps
AAH   Advanced Attack Helicopter
ABC   Advancing Blade Concept
Ac   Altocumulus
A/C   Aircraft
ADF   Automatic Direction Finder
ADR   Advisory Route
AFCS   Automatic Flight Control System
AGL   Above Ground Level
AIS   Aeronautical Information Service
ALT   Altitude
ASA   Advisory Service Area
ASH   Advanced Scout Helicopter
ASI   Air Speed Indicator
ASR   Altimeter Setting Region
ASW   Anti-Submarine Warfare
ATAFCS   Airborne Target Acquisition and Fire Control System
ATW   Anti Tank Warfare
BAH   British Airways Helicopters
BD   Blade Damper
BHAB   British Helicopter Advisory Board
BHL Bristow Helicopters Limited
BI   Blade Inspection

BL   Blade Loading
BRG   Bearing
CAA   Civil Aviation Authority
CAC   Collective Acceleration Control
CE   Coriolis Effect
CF   Centrifugal Force
CG   Centre of Gravity
CHD   Chord
C of A   Certificate of Airworthiness
C of P   Centre of Pressure
CPC   Collective Pitch Control Cyclic Pitch Control
CPL(H)   Commercial Pilots Licence (Helicopters)
C/S   Call Sign
DA   Density Altitude Disc Area
DALR   Dry Adiabatic Lapse Rate
DF   Direction Finding
DGI   Directional Gyro Indicator
DH   Delta Hinge
DL   Disc Loading
DME   Distance Measuring Equipment
DOL   Dissymmetry of Lift
DR   Dead Reckoning
FA   Feathering Axis or Feathering Action

FAA Fleet Air Arm or (US) Federal Aviation Administration
FAS Force Adjustment System
FIR Flight Information Region
FIS Flight Information Service
FL Flight Level
GC Great Circle
GE Ground Effect
GP Gyroscopic Precession
G/S Ground Speed
HELCIS Helicopter Command Instrument System
HF High Frequency
HHI Hughes Helicopters Incorporated
HIGE Hovering In Ground Effect
HLH Heavy Lift Helicopter
HOGE Hovering out of Ground Effect
IAS Indicated Airspeed
IFR Instrument Flight Rules
IMC Instrument Meteorological Conditions
ISA International Standard Atmosphere
ISIS Integrated Spar Inspection System
Kc/S Kilocycles Per Second
Kt Knot
LAMPS Light Airborne Multi-Purpose System
LASSIE Low Airspeed Sensing and Indicating Equipment
Ldg Wt Leading Weight
LOH Light Observation Helicopter
MAMCH Manned Anti-Surface Missile Carrying Helicopter
MARS Mid Air Recovery System
MATCH Manned Anti-Submarine Torpedo Carrying Helicopter
MATZ Military Air Traffic Zone
MBB Messerschmitt-Bölkow-Blohm
Min Minute

MM Middle Marker
MSL Mean Sea Level
NDB Non-Directional Beacon
NOE Nap-of-the-Earth
NS Nimbostratus
OCL Obstacle Clearance Limit
OM Outer Marker
PA Pitch Angle
PADS Position and Azimuth Determining System
PE Pressure Error
RAS Rectified Airspeed
RAST Recovery Assist Secure and Traverse
RB Relative Bearing
RCC Rescue Co-ordination System
RPH Remotely-Piloted Helicopter
RPV Remotely-Piloted Vehicle
RR Rigid Rotor
RSRA Rotor Systems Research Aircraft
RVR Reversing Velocity Rotor
SALR Saturated Adiabatic Lapse Rate
SAR Search And Rescue
SAS Stability Augmentation System
SR Solidity Ratio
SRR/FLIR Short Range Recovery/Forward Looking Infra-Red System
SRZ Special Rules Zone
STALP Ship Tethered Aerial Lifting Programme
TADS/PNVS Target Acquisition Display System/Pilot's Night Vision System
TL Translational Lift
TMA Terminal Control Area
TPP Tip Path Plane
TR Track
TS Tip Speed or Tip Stall
TX Transmitter
UKAP United Kingdom Aeronautical Publication

UTTAS   Utility Tactical Transport Aircraft System

VDR   Variable Diameter Rotor

VFR   Visual Flight Rules

VMC   Visual Meteorological Conditions

VOR   Very High Frequency Omni-Directional Range

W/S   Wind Speed

W/V   Wind Velocity

Bibliography

Aircraft of the Royal Navy, Paul Ellis (Jane's); *Aircraft Aircraft*, John W.R. Taylor (Hamlyn); *Aircraft of the RAF: A Pictorial Record 1918–1978*, John W.R. Taylor (Macdonald & Jane's); *Air Rescue*, Lt Cols Carroll Gliness & Wendell F. Moseley (Ace Books Inc); *Angels without Wings*, Peter Whittle & Michael Borissow (Angley Book Company Ltd); *All About Helicopters*, Jean Ross Howard (Sports Car Press); *British Naval Aircraft Since 1912*, Owen Thetford (Putnam); *Basic Helicopter Handbook*, Dale Crane (Aviation Maintenance Publishers); *Civil Airliner Recognition*, John W.R. Taylor (Ian Allan); *Chickenhawk*, Robert Mason (Corgi); *Flashing Blades Over The Sea*, Lt Cdr J.M. Milne RN (Maritime Books); *Flying For Fun*, Keith Carey (Patrick Stephens Ltd); *Gunslingers in Action*, Lou Drendel (Squadron/Signal Publications); *Helicopters and VTOL Aircraft Work Like This*, Basil Arkell & John W.R. Taylor (J.M. Dent & Sons Ltd); *Helicopters of the World*, Bill Gunston (Aerospace Publishing); *Helicopters & Other Rotorcraft Since 1907*, Kenneth Munson (Blandford Press Ltd); *Helicopters of the World*, Michael Taylor & John W.R. Taylor (Ian Allan); *Helicopters Guide to Military Rotorcraft*, Bill Gunston (Salamander); *Helicopter Design & Data Manual*, S.J. Dzik (Aviation Publications); *Helicopters At War*, Bill Gunston (Hamlyn); *Helicopter Rescue*, John Chartres (Ian Allan); *Illustrated History of Aircraft*, Brendan Gallagher (Treasure Press); *Jane's All The World's Aircraft*, John W.R. Taylor (Jane's); *Jane's World Aircraft Recognition Handbook*, Derek Wood (Jane's); *Kitty Hawk To Concorde*, H.F. King & John W.R. Taylor (Hamlyn); *Soldiers In The Air*, Peter Mead (Ian Allan); *The British Army In Ulster*, David Barzilay (Century Books); *The Helicopter*, John Fay (David & Charles); *The Helicopter Directory*, Joseph Mill Brown (David & Charles).

Magazines and journals
Air Pictorial; Aviation News; Air Extra; Aircraft Illustrated; Airtour Gazette; Armed Forces; Air International; Aeroplane Monthly; Battle; Flying; Flight International; Helicopter International; Pilot; Rotor & Wing; Royal Air Force Yearbook.

Index